Great Year-Round
GRILLING
in the
SOUTHWEST

Great Year-Round GRILLING in the SOUTHWEST

The Flavors • The Culinary Traditions • The Techniques

Ellen Brown

The Lyons Press
Guilford, Connecticut
An Imprint of The Globe Pequot Press

To buy books in quantity for corporate use
or incentives, call **(800) 962–0973**
or e-mail **premiums@GlobePequot.com**.

The Lyons Press is an imprint of The Globe Pequot Press

Photos on the following pages courtesy of Shutterstock: 1, 3, 8, 9, 10, 11, 21, 26, 28, 33, 40, 49, 53, 61, 63, 70, 75, 79, 83, 86, 93, 94, 96, 102, 106, 113, 115, 118

Photos on the following pages courtesy of Jupiterimages: xi, 2, 5, 17, 31, 34, 37, 44, 47, 50, 55, 56, 64, 68, 98, 100, 103, 109

Photos on page xii courtesy of the Library of Congress

Text design by Sheryl Kober

Library of Congress Cataloging-in-Publication Data

Brown, Ellen.
    Great year-round grilling in the Southwest : the flavors—the culinary traditions—the techniques / Ellen Brown.
      p. cm.
    ISBN 978-1-59921-485-6
    1. Barbecue cookery—Southwestern States 2. Cookery, American—Southwestern style. I. Title.
    TX840.B3B75788 2009
    641.5'7840976--dc22
                                                                                2008042719

Printed in China

10 9 8 7 6 5 4 3 2 1

This book is dedicated to Lisa Cerami and Josh Dubler, with my love and hopes that their life together will always be as spicy as a jalapeño and as colorful as a desert sunset.

Contents

Chapter 1: **Grilling Fundamentals** 1

This chapter includes everything you need to know about grills and grilling to successfully cook all the recipes in the book, beginning with the principles of grilling; charcoal vs. gas grills; accessories for ease and safety; grilling safety; how to gauge when the grill is ready to cook; how to use wood chips to add smoky flavor to foods; and how to create multi-level fires.

Chapter 2: **Ways to Flavor Food: Rubs, Pastes, Marinades, and Brines** 7

There are basically four ways to flavor food destined for the grill—rubs, pastes, marinades, and brines—and the amount of time required to impart flavor ranges from seconds to days. Some recipes in this chapter include flavors from the Southwest, while others encompass other regions of American cooking as well as cuisines from around the world.

Chapter 3: **Sauces for Basting and Topping** 17

This chapter includes sauces to dress up grilled food and elevate a simple entree to a dish of distinction. These sauces are versatile, and can go with many types of food; each recipe is annotated with the categories of grilled food with which it is compatible.

Chapter 4: **Hors d'Oeuvres and Appetizers** 25

Grilled hors d'oeuvres are as varied as slices of toasted bruschetta topped with fresh tomatoes and Thai chicken satay with peanut sauce. What differentiates hors d'oeuvres from appetizers is that the former are "finger food" and can be eaten without a plate and fork.

Chapter 5: **Soups and Small Vegetable Salads** 32

From the corn in Tex-Mex Tortilla Soup to all the vegetables in Farmer's Market Vegetable Soup, grilling adds its flavor to the main ingredients that go into soups, and in the same way, small salads can be topped with grilled fare or include grilled ingredients. The salads in this chapter are small appetizers rather than the larger entree salads of Chapter 11.

Contents

roasted in a relatively cool oven to complete cooking without drying out the outer layers of meat, while others begin by being seared or smoked on the grill and are then braised to that wonderful term—fork tender. The chapter begins with charts on how to time foods cooked by these methods.

Thin-crust pizzas cooked on the grill can be topped with myriad ingredients, some with Southwestern flavors. The chapter includes a foolproof recipe for basic pizza dough, with various recipes for topping it.

If a grill is lit, it seems senseless to use another cooking method for complementary components of the meal. Grilled vegetables are as varied as kebabs of peppers and onion and heads of radicchio and that greatest of all summer treats—farm-fresh corn. Some of these recipes can also be served as vegetarian entrees.

While this book includes recipes for vegetables and other side dishes cooked on the grill, many times the grill is reserved for the entree while the supporting players are created in the kitchen. Condiments like salsa and guacamole are commonly served with all Tex-Mex and other Southwestern dishes, as are variations on beans. Many of these foods star in this chapter's recipes.

The title of this chapter is not an oxymoron, nor is it just variations on toasted marshmallow—although it includes a recipe for S'mores. The grill is a natural way to glean the most luscious flavor from fruit, because heating enhances the fruits' natural sweetness as well as creating a softer texture. Fruit desserts comprise the majority of these recipes.

Creamy flan as well as fruit and chocolate are hallmarks of desserts in the Southwestern states; in this chapter you will find them all represented. Interspersed are recipes for dishes that are national favorites—from Strawberry Shortcake to a variety of cookies and other sweet treats.

Preface

To me, grilling is more than a way of cooking; it's a way of life. The process of grilling food arouses so many sensual pleasures that the end result is more than just a meal. Perhaps that is the reason why I grill year-round; the aroma of food cooking on the grill is as welcome when bundled up against the January cold as it is when lounging in the balmy breezes of July.

Grilling is hardly an exact science; every fire, even one ignited on a gas grill, is different, just as every piece of food cooked on it is unique. The temperature of the air, the velocity and direction of the wind, and the relative humidity all have to be factored into how long it will take a grill to heat and how long it will take food to cook on it. That means that your eyes play a major role when grilling to judge what "done" means, as you poke at food to judge its texture. The sound of food searing adds aural expectation to the experience, and then there's the aroma—emerging not just from the grill but also from the food itself as the steam rises from the plate and reaches the nose.

Grilling, more than any other cooking method, provides an opportunity to share the process with those who will benefit from the results. While a few friends might keep me company in the kitchen from time to time, conventional cooking is basically a solitary endeavor. But a grill becomes the center of a social event, and hovering around it while chatting or sipping is anticipation of a meal that both the cook and the guests can enjoy. Grilling is part of Americans' way of life, be it limited to the summer months in some states and year-round in others.

Most of my personal grilling has taken place in the Northeast. I currently live in Rhode Island, but I grilled on beaches and decks on Nantucket for more than a decade prior to moving here, lit many grills in tiny Georgetown courtyards while living in Washington, and spent childhood summers grilling on the sandy shores of Long Island.

However, I've traveled extensively researching American cuisine during the past twenty-five years, both its historic roots and contemporary manifestations; much of this travel was to the Southwest to write a book entitled *Southwest Tastes*, which was the companion volume to the trailblazing television series *Great Chefs of the West*.

While trekking from lush beaches of the Texas coast on the Gulf of Mexico to the arid mountains of New Mexico and Colorado for almost a year, I became immersed in the flavors of food in the Southwest as well as its vibrant colors and deeply rooted history. As is the case with all American regional cuisines, dishes developed based on the prototypes brought by immigrants when combined with available foods.

But this early culinary history has been tempered by the waves of immigrants who arrived from the nineteenth to twenty-first centuries, and as the size and scope of our larders have increased exponentially with air travel and modern agricultural practices. That is why there are so many international dishes along with traditional American foods in this book; it is those foods that reflect the America of today and the various ethnic heritages that are now blended into those of the original settlers.

I hope you enjoy grilling the dishes in this book, and I hope that as you grill them you allow the pleasures of grilling to become a larger part of your life.

Ellen Brown
Providence, Rhode Island

While writing a book is a solitary endeavor, its publication is always a team effort. My thanks go to:

Eugene Brissie of The Lyons Press for envisioning such an exciting project.

Ed Claflin, my agent, for his constant support and great humor.

The talented staff at The Lyons Press, especially to Ellen Urban for her knowledgeable editorial guidance, Diana Nuhn for the crash course she provided on photo selection, Sheryl Kober for her inspired design, and Jane Crosen for her eagle-eyed editing.

Constance Brown and Kenn Speiser, my dear neighbors and friends, who good-heartedly ignored the constant smoke from my grills wafting into their backyard from mine.

My many friends whose palates and culinary savvy aided me in recipe development, most especially my beloved sister, Nancy Dubler.

Tigger and Patches, my furry companions, who personally endorse all fish and seafood dishes.

Introduction

The History of Food Traditions in the Southwestern States

Traditional Southwestern cuisine, with its assertive clear flavors and bright colors, evolved more by circumstances than design. It is the result of the serendipity that led Spanish, Mexican, and Anglo settlers to a region of what is now the United States where a Native American civilization was already flourishing.

Crops unknown to the Spanish—corn, squash, and beans—became the basis for the region's larder. The Spanish brought the seedlings for previously unknown fruit trees, and received the chile pepper in return.

The geographic isolation of Southwestern settlements allowed such pockets of ethnicity to flourish. Within the array of Southwest flavors, there are subcultures that transcend regional variations. The chuck wagon cookery that nourished the cowboys, those modern nomads so romanticized in folklore, developed wherever they were herding cattle to market.

Another constant, regardless of the meats or seasonings used, was the barbecue. The word barbecue is derived from the Spanish word *barbacoa*, which, in turn, came from the Native American word for a framework of green wood used to support meat or fish over the coals. While grilling, the oldest form of cooking, has come of age and is now sophisticated, it originated in this method of long cooking over low heat, which was used by Native American tribes from Canada to the Patagonian pampas.

The backbone of their cuisine was corn, supplemented by beans for protein and by chiles, squash, and tomatoes for taste and vitamins. The gathering of corn is still celebrated by the Hopi, the Pueblo tribe of Arizona, at Niman, the most important *kachina* ceremony of the season. It forms the basis for *piki*, the brittle Indian bread that is the predecessor of the tortilla.

And the all-important tortilla, which we now know as the bread for Southwestern and Mexican cookery, was an Indian invention. The Pueblo tribe used blue corn more often than any other of the brightly colored species they raised, and they had a fascination with the color blue in general. Anthropologists credit this to a parallel made with the benevolence of the blue sky.

The topography of Texas differentiates it from other states in the Southwest. It is important to recall that unlike New Mexico and Arizona, Texas has a 375-mile stretch of coastline on the Gulf of Mexico, and the most important commodity gleaned from the waters is shrimp.

Equally distinctive as Texas cookery are the dishes native to New Mexico. Long the domain of the Pueblo Indians, New Mexico was settled by Spaniards moving north from Mexico, who began to establish outposts after the first forays by Spanish explorer Francisco de Coronado in 1540. They had moved along the Rio

Tortillas, shown cooking, developed from the flatbreads made by Native Americans.

In 1903, President Teddy Roosevelt enjoyed a chuck wagon breakfast with cowboys in Hugo, Colorado.

Grande by 1598, only to find they were virtually isolated from the rest of the world by the desert and frequently hostile Native American tribes.

It was nearly a century later that fifteen hundred colonists emigrated to Santa Fe, and El Camino Real, the colonial counterpart of an interstate highway, secured contact between the capital of New Mexico and Mexico City. The ranchos they built showed the mark of European parentage: orchards of apple, apricot, and peach trees as well as vineyards.

While settling New Mexico was a goal of the Spanish, they virtually ignored the adjoining land of Arizona for a century longer, until the advent of large-scale copper mining and cattle raising made settlement of the territory advantageous.

In general, Arizona food is based on the cooking of Sonora, the desert section of Mexico right across the border. It is milder than the cuisine of most Mexican provinces; many dishes contain no chiles at all, and flour rather than corn tortillas are the norm.

These three states are the major sources of Southwest traditional cooking. States such as Colorado, which was settled centuries later and lacked the synergistic blending of cultures, made few contributions to Southwest tastes. The variations of dishes in that state are due more to ingredient availability than cultural influences.

Utah and Nevada were also settled much later. The discovery of the Comstock Lode at what became Virginia City, Nevada, in 1859 brought with it a huge migration of prospectors and made this outpost a cosmopolitan enclave where wealthy mine owners would import champagne and chefs from France to cook in their homes and private clubs. Oklahoma's culinary heritage was also later to develop. The area shared Native American tribes with the states of the Great Plains more than with the other Southwestern states. The homesteading of Oklahoma did not begin until 1889, and the majority of the homesteaders were small farmers from the Midwest and South who brought those food traditions with them.

The plains of the desert gave rise to a new category of nomadic people once the Native Americans had been settled on their reservations. What the famed cowboys of the nineteenth century, such as Kit Carson and Doc Holliday, had in common with their less celebrated compatriots was the school of chuck wagon cookery.

The first chuck wagons, dating to right after the Civil War, were two- and four-wheeled vehicles drawn by oxen, mules, or horses; the contents were stowed and covered with hides or tarpaulins. Chuck was slang for food, or "grub," and the wagon served as a kitchen on the move. The key to its design was a large device called the chuck box, set at the wagon's rear, with a back that swung down like a tailgate of a station wagon to become a work surface where the "cookie" or "coosie" (from the Spanish word *cocinero*, for cook) would work, preparing beans for a pot nestled in the ashes or ready to grill simple foods over the fire.

Most of the chuck wagon cooks were older cowboys who still had the stamina to rise long before dawn. Lore has it that these cooks ruled their camps with a hand as hard as their cast-iron skillets. An old proverb in the Southwest says: "Only a damned fool would argue with a skunk, a woman, or a roundup cook."

The discovery of gold brought settlers in search of the Comstock Lode in 1859.

Chapter 1

Grilling Fundamentals

The unifying factor to most of the recipes in this book—excluding many desserts and side dishes—is that at some point food comes into contact with a grill. This chapter introduces you to the basic equipment and techniques used when grilling food.

Charcoal Grills

All charcoal grills have two grates; the lower grate holds the charcoal and the upper grate holds the food. Charcoal briquettes or pieces of hardwood charcoal rest on the lower grate, and once they are lit you can move them around to create the heat pattern that is best for each recipe.

The temperature of the fire is controlled by opening and closing the top and bottom vents. The more these vents are open, the hotter the fire will be, and the more they are closed, the cooler the fire.

Charcoal briquettes are the fuel used overwhelmingly by charcoal grillers, accounting for almost 90 percent of the charcoal purchased in 2007. Invented by automotive pioneer Henry Ford, briquettes are made of low-quality, powdered charcoal and binders that are compressed and molded into little black pillows.

An alternative to briquettes is hardwood charcoal, created by burning hardwood in a furnace using very little oxygen. A piece of hardwood charcoal is almost pure carbon, and has neither glue nor additives

Unlike conventional cooking, grills can be set up anywhere—including on secluded coves.

One of the great twentieth-century innovations was the covered kettle grill.

briquettes that are pre-soaked with lighter fluid so only lighting is necessary. My suggestion is to start with ten to twelve pre-soaked briquettes, and once they are flaming, add conventional charcoal on top. Your food is less likely to develop the petroleum taste associated with lighter fluid.

- **Chimney charcoal lighter.** These are becoming increasingly popular because they do not involve petroleum, but they are a problem to take along for a cookout away from the house because of their bulky size. They are essentially a metal tube with a handle on one side. Inside is a grate to hold the charcoal and a chamber underneath for crumpled newspaper. Light the newspaper using a match or lighter, and set the chimney on the grill grate. The chimney effect takes the newspaper's flames up through the charcoal and lights it. When a white ash forms on the charcoal, pour the lighted coals out onto the charcoal grate.

present. While almost double the cost of generic briquettes, it does burn hotter and the fire can be controlled more effectively than if you use briquettes.

Starting a charcoal fire is hardly difficult, and depending on how many accoutrements you want to buy, you can accomplish the job with very little effort. Here is a summary of the primary ways charcoal fires are lit:

- **Lighter fluid.** This petroleum product is very volatile, and should be used with extreme caution. Arrange charcoal in a pyramid in the center of your grill, and spray the coals evenly with the fluid until saturated. Allow the liquid to penetrate for 1 minute, and then light the coals in locations all around the base of the pyramid with a long match or a long-handled butane lighter. *Never use additional lighter fluid once the coals have been initially lit and are smoldering.*

- **Self-starting charcoal briquettes.** These are

Charcoal briquettes are stacked up in a chimney starter, with newspaper stuffed into the bottom chamber for fuel.

Tips for All Charcoal Grills

While charcoal grills range from small ones designed for picnics to ones encased in extravagant outdoor kitchens, certain rules apply. The key to success when grilling over charcoal is how well the fire is built, and then how well it is maintained if grilling for a long duration. Here are some considerations for all charcoal fires:

- **Use enough charcoal.** This is perhaps the most common foible of charcoal grilling, regardless if the food to be grilled is a lowly hot dog or a luxurious tenderloin of beef. Make sure the fire is 4 inches larger in diameter than the food to be cooked over it. The higher the charcoal is banked, the hotter the fire will be. If you want to cook over a very hot fire, build the coals to within 3 inches of the grate on which the food will cook. Determine the amount of charcoal you need by piling it up under the cooking grate, and then push it into a pyramid for easy lighting or place it in a chimney.

- **Make sure the charcoal is ready.** Whether using briquettes or hardwood charcoal, the visual sign is that all pieces are lightly covered with gray ash. This means that the charcoal is fully lit and hot.

- **Clean out the ashes regularly.** The heat of a charcoal fire can be diminished if the bottom vents of the grill are clogged with ashes. Remove both grates, close the bottom vents, and scoop out the ashes. Remember to open the vents before lighting the next batch of charcoal.

- **Close down the grill after cooking.** There is no reason to waste charcoal, so close the top and bottom vents on the grill to shut it off. The half-used charcoal can be placed off to the side and used to refresh the next fire.

Gas Grills

There is no question that a gas grill is more convenient than cooking with charcoal. Lighting a gas grill is like lighting the oven broiler, and gas grills offer unparalleled convenience. Many people believe, however, that what is lost is some of the flavor and aroma transferred to food when cooking on a charcoal grill.

Gas grills use natural or LP gas for heat and flames, so the fire is efficient. Here is how to light most of them, although you should always consult the manufacturer's instructions: Open the cover, and then open the valve of the gas tank. One at a time, turn the controls to high and ignite the corresponding burner with either a long butane lighter, a long match, or the burner's own electronic ignition. Close the cover and wait 15 to 20 minutes for your grill to reach its highest heat.

Stopping a gas grill is just as easy as lighting one. Turn off each burner, and close off the gas valve. Then turn one of the burners on high for 15 seconds to bleed any gas remaining in the line, turn that burner off, and close the cover.

Tips for All Gas Grills

Gas grills are convenient, but there are also some innate safety problems because you are cooking with a highly volatile liquid. Here are some considerations for safety as well as achieving the best flavor:

- **Always keep the lid down except if expressly told to leave it open in a recipe.** Gas burns cleanly, so no residue accumulates on the interior of the lid from high-heat cooking.

- **Remove the warming rack, assuming the grill has one, before lighting the grill.** Unless you plan to actually use it, the warming rack gets in the way of turning food at the back of the grate, and can burn your hand as you try.

- **Do not skimp on the preheating time.** It is easy to know when a charcoal fire is ready for cooking, but with a gas grill your only clue is how long it has been heating. Give it a full 15 minutes, and longer in cold weather.

- **Store propane tanks—full or empty—in a well-ventilated space.** They should never be placed in a garage or basement.

Gas grills are becoming increasingly popular due to the convenience of merely turning on a burner.

Grilling Accessories

Gourmet shops and Web sites are filled with grilling accessories, but there are only a few that are really necessary. Here is a brief list of ones I find useful:

- **Spray bottle.** For problems to be serious enough that a fire extinguisher is necessary is not common; however, minor flare-ups caused by fat dripping onto either charcoal or metal bars are a routine occurrence when grilling. A spray bottle—either purchased for the grill or a well-washed-out one from a cleaning product—is important to keep around at all times. You can target the flames without disturbing the food above them.

- **Stainless-steel tongs.** You should have a few pairs of tongs, with handles at least 12 inches long. Use tongs and not a meat fork for turning food (a meat fork causes food to lose juice and become dry).

- **Spatula.** A long-handled spatula makes flipping hamburgers and moving other foods easy.

- **Grill brush.** Use a grill brush to clean the grate on which the food sits. I clean it once at the end of grilling, and then again before adding food the next time.

- **Instant-read thermometer.** This piece of inexpensive equipment should be mandatory in every kitchen, not only for grilling but for roasting as well. All you have to do is stick it into the thickest part of food and leave it in for 20 seconds, and it registers an accurate reading on the doneness of your food.

Long handles are the primary requirement for cooking tools used at the grill.

• **Metal and bamboo skewers.** While metal skewers are indestructible, they are not as aesthetically pleasing as delicate ones made from bamboo.

Using Wood Chips for Flavor

Wood chips made from aromatic woods like hickory, mesquite, apple, and cherry add immeasurably to the flavor of grilled foods, as well as giving the skin of poultry a rich mahogany color. For charcoal grills, the secret is to soak the chips in water to cover for at least 30 minutes. Even though they do not create as pronounced a flavor, you can also use wood chips on a gas grill. Place about 2 cups dry wood chips in the center of a large (12 x 18-inch) piece of heavy-duty aluminum foil. Bring up the foil on all sides and roll the ends together to seal the pouch. Poke several small holes in the top of the packet. Once the grill is hot, place the wood chip pouch under the grate across the burner shields. Smoke will eventually emerge from the holes.

Fire Configurations for Grilling

Each recipe in this book contains information about the appropriate temperature and configuration of the grill for the success of the recipe. This section guides you through what each of these mean.

• **Direct grilling.** This was how all grilling was accomplished prior to the invention of the covered kettle grill and the gas grill. The coals are lit and then evenly spread three to four layers deep on the lower grate.

• **Dual-temperature grilling.** Once the coals are ignited and have reached the desired temperature, you can customize the fire to the needs of the food. By spreading the coals so that they are three or four deep on one side of the grill and one or two layers deep on the other side, you can sear food and then transfer it to the cooler side to complete the cooking. For a gas grill, preheat the grill on high, and then reduce half the burners to MEDIUM.

- **Indirect grilling.** When you are cooking by indirect heat on a charcoal grill, what you are actually doing is turning your covered grill into an outdoor oven. The coals are pushed to the periphery of the grill and the food is placed in the center over an aluminum drip pan rather than over direct heat. The grill is always kept covered, and the top and bottom vents are partially closed. If you have a gas grill with more than one burner, it is possible to cook over indirect heat. The grills best suited to indirect cooking are those with right and left rather than front and back burners.

Determining the Temperature of a Grill

After the coals have a light coating of ash or the gas burners have been preheated, place your hand, palm-side down, about 4–5 inches above the cooking rack, and count slowly. Here are your readings to determine the temperature of the grill.

- Hot grill: 2 seconds

- Medium-hot grill: 3–4 seconds

- Medium grill: 5–6 seconds

- Medium-low grill: 7 seconds

Grilling is a high-heat cooking method, so if you can hold your hand over the coals for more than 7 seconds, it means you should be adding more coals or preheating the gas burners longer.

Preparing the Grill Grate

Once the grill grate has heated from the fire, take a stiff wire grill brush and brush it well to remove any cooked-on food remaining.

Treating the grate with oil just prior to grilling helps ensure that food will not stick. The best way to do this is to dip a paper towel in vegetable oil, and then, holding it with tongs, rub it all over the grill grate. This is an important step to good grilling.

The Timing of Recipes and How to Use This Book

There is no universal style of cookbook and recipe writing; each author approaches the task in a somewhat personal way. In order to provide you with the maximum number of recipes, the preparation of the fire refers you back to this chapter rather than using space to restate it constantly.

Each recipe is annotated with the number of servings, which is usually given as a range. If the dish is part of a multi-course meal, it can be "stretched" to feed more people; if it is an item that is one-per-person, the number of servings is finite.

"Active time," the second annotation, is the amount of hands-on prep time needed in the kitchen before food goes to the grill. In almost all cases the amount is less than 25 minutes, or less than the amount of time needed for a charcoal grill to heat properly. This is the time measurement for all the chopping, dicing, and indoor cooking.

The third annotation is "Start to finish." While grilling is a cooking method that can be considered "fast food" because it cooks with high heat, the time needed to properly light and heat the grill must always be factored into the equation; it may take only 5 minutes to cook a pounded chicken breast, but that is after the grill is ready to accomplish the task.

The recipes in this book are calculated to factor in the fire preparation as part of the time necessary to complete the dish, and to be on the safe side, the assumption is 25–30 minutes.

Chapter 2

Ways to Flavor Food:
Rubs, Pastes, Marinades, and Brines

There are basically four ways to flavor food before it goes on the grill—rubs, pastes, marinades, and brines—and the amount of time required to impart flavor ranges from seconds to days. In this chapter you will find recipes for all these ways to treat food destined for the grill.

Rubs

Rubs are a relatively new addition to the arsenal of ways to flavor foods, and they truly do offer flavor without fuss. Most rubs are highly concentrated mixtures of dried herbs and spices that should be applied to food after it has been brushed with oil. And "rub" is what you should do. Rather than just giving food a light sprinkle, the mixture should be rubbed into the food with your fingertips, at which time it is ready to be grilled.

Tex-Mex Rub

Yield: ½ cup | Active time: 5 minutes | Start to finish: 5 minutes | Uses: All foods

Combine chili powder, paprika, cumin, coriander, garlic powder, oregano, black pepper, and red pepper flakes in a bowl, and mix well. Store in an airtight container in a cool, dry place for up to 1 month.

2 tablespoons chili powder
2 tablespoons paprika
1 tablespoon ground cumin
1 tablespoon ground coriander
1 tablespoon garlic powder
1 tablespoon dried oregano
1 teaspoon freshly ground black pepper
1 teaspoon crushed red pepper flakes

Coffee Chili Rub

Yield: 1/3 cup | Active time: 5 minutes | Start to finish: 5 minutes | Uses: Beef, lamb, chicken

Combine chili powder, coffee powder, brown sugar, mustard, and pepper in a bowl, and mix well. Store in an airtight container in a cool, dry place for up to 1 month.

4 tablespoons chili powder
2 tablespoons instant espresso coffee powder
1 tablespoon firmly packed dark brown sugar
2 teaspoons dry mustard
1 teaspoon freshly ground black pepper

3 tablespoons paprika

2 tablespoons garlic powder

1 tablespoon onion powder

1 tablespoon dried oregano

1 tablespoon dried thyme

2 teaspoons freshly ground black pepper

1 teaspoon cayenne

Creole Rub

Yield: ½ cup | Active time: 5 minutes | Start to finish: 5 minutes | Uses: All foods

Combine paprika, garlic powder, onion powder, oregano, thyme, pepper, and cayenne in a bowl, and mix well. Store in an airtight container in a cool, dry place for up to 1 month.

3 tablespoons dry mustard

2 tablespoon garlic powder

2 tablespoons coarsely ground black pepper

1 tablespoon dried oregano

2 teaspoons dried basil

Steakhouse-Style Rub

Yield: ½ cup | Active time: 5 minutes | Start to finish: 5 minutes | Uses: Beef, lamb

Combine mustard, garlic powder, pepper, oregano, and basil in a bowl, and mix well. Store in an airtight container in a cool, dry place for up to 1 month.

Spices such as peppercorns and fennel seeds should be crushed in a mortar and pestle to release their flavor.

Spices are used around the world and add vibrant color as well as flavor to foods.

Spanish Spice Rub

Yield: ½ cup | Active time: 5 minutes | Start to finish: 5 minutes | Uses: All foods

Combine paprika, cumin, mustard, turmeric, and oregano in a bowl, and mix well. Store in an airtight container in a cool, dry place for up to 1 month.

6 tablespoons Spanish smoked paprika

2 tablespoons ground cumin

1 tablespoon dry mustard

1 tablespoon ground turmeric

1 tablespoon dried oregano

Aromatic Herb and Spice Rub

Yield: ½ cup | Active time: 5 minutes | Start to finish: 5 minutes | Uses: All foods

Combine coriander, thyme, cumin, pepper, oregano, and sage in a bowl, and mix well. Store in an airtight container in a cool, dry place for up to 1 month.

2 tablespoons ground coriander

2 tablespoons dried thyme

1 tablespoon ground cumin

1 tablespoon freshly ground black pepper

1 tablespoon dried oregano

1 tablespoon dried sage

Basic Herb Rub

Yield: ½ cup | Active time: 5 minutes | Start to finish: 5 minutes | Uses: All foods

Combine rosemary, thyme, sage, tarragon, and pepper in a bowl, and mix well. Store in an airtight container in a cool, dry place for up to 1 month.

3 tablespoons crumbled dried rosemary

3 tablespoons dried thyme

3 tablespoons dried sage

1 tablespoon dried tarragon

1 tablespoon freshly ground black pepper

Pastes

Pastes represent the middle ground between rubs and marinades, and the amount of time needed to use them is more than a rub but less than a marinade. Pastes are highly concentrated in the same way as rubs, but they also contain some perishable ingredients for accent flavors, so they are moist. Many pastes have oil added to create the proper thick texture. They should be rubbed onto meat, and allowed to sit for at least 20 minutes, or about the same amount of time it takes for a grill to heat.

---

3 tablespoons dried tarragon

2 tablespoons dried thyme

2 tablespoons grated lemon zest

4 garlic cloves, peeled and pressed through a garlic press

2 teaspoons freshly ground black pepper

3 tablespoons olive oil

Lemon-Herb Paste

Yield: ½ cup | Active time: 10 minutes | Start to finish: 10 minutes | Uses: Chicken, fish and seafood, pork, veal

Combine tarragon, thyme, lemon zest, garlic, and pepper in a bowl, and mix well. Add oil, and mix into a paste. Store in an airtight container, refrigerated, for up to 3 days.

Fresh herbs add their aroma and color to pastes and marinades.

To preserve both color and potency, spices should be kept in a cool, dry, dark place.

Tandoori Paste

Yield: ½ cup | Active time: 10 minutes | Start to finish: 10 minutes | Uses: Beef, lamb, chicken, fish and seafood

Combine ginger, garlic, cumin, turmeric, cardamom, and cayenne in a bowl, and mix well. Add oil, and mix into a paste. Store in an airtight container, refrigerated, for up to 3 days.

3 tablespoons grated fresh ginger

5 garlic cloves, peeled and pressed through a garlic press

2 tablespoons ground cumin

2 tablespoons turmeric

1 tablespoon ground cardamom

½ teaspoon cayenne

4 tablespoons olive oil

Moroccan Paste

Yield: 1 cup | Active time: 10 minutes | Start to finish: 10 minutes | Uses: Fish and seafood, chicken

Combine parsley, cilantro, garlic, cumin, paprika, lemon zest, and red pepper flakes in a bowl, and mix well. Add oil and lemon juice, and mix into a paste. Store in an airtight container, refrigerated, for up to 3 days.

½ cup chopped fresh parsley

½ cup chopped fresh cilantro

6 garlic cloves, peeled and pressed through a garlic press

1 tablespoon ground cumin

1 tablespoon paprika

1 teaspoon grated lemon zest

Crushed red pepper flakes to taste

⅓ cup olive oil

2 tablespoons freshly squeezed lemon juice

Marinades

Marinades are a time-honored stalwart of cooking. If given enough time, food will definitely absorb the flavor, and marinades can also render less expensive cuts of meat buttery tender. To tenderize, some sort of acid must be present. Vinegars, with the exception of rice wine and balsamic, are too strong; wines and citrus juices are far more delicate, and the food will have a complex flavor from the combination of ingredients rather than having any one dominate.

The following chart will give you some general guidelines to marinating different types of food. Keep in mind that the thinner the food, the less time is needed to achieve a meaningful flavor. Also, heartier foods require longer than delicate foods.

Marinating Foods: How Much and for How Long		
FOOD	LIQUID PER POUND	TIME
Beef	½ cup	3–24 hours
Lamb	½ cup	3–24 hours
Pork	½ cup	2–12 hours
Veal	½ cup	1–3 hours
Chicken, with skin and bones	⅓ cup	4–12 hours
Chicken breasts, boneless and skinless	⅓ cup	30 minutes–3 hours
Turkey, whole	1 cup	24 hours
Turkey breast cutlets	⅓ cup	30 minutes–3 hours
Duck, whole	½ cup	4–24 hours
Delicately flavored fish fillets (sole, halibut) and shellfish	¼ cup	30 minutes
Strongly flavored fish fillets/steaks (tuna, bluefish)	¼–½ cup	30 minutes–1 hour
Tender vegetables (mushrooms)	¼ cup	1–2 hours
Thick-skinned vegetables (peppers, eggplant)	¼ cup	2–4 hours

Tex-Mex Fajita Marinade

Yield: ¾ cup | Active time: 10 minutes | Start to finish: 10 minutes | Uses: Beef, chicken

Combine lime juice, tequila, chile, garlic, lime zest, salt, and pepper in a heavy resealable plastic bag, and mix well. Add oil, and mix well again. Add food to be marinated, turning the bag to coat food evenly. Marinate food according to chart above.

Note: The marinade can be refrigerated for up to 3 days, tightly covered.

¼ cup freshly squeezed lime juice

3 tablespoons tequila

1 jalapeño or serrano chile, seeds and ribs removed, and finely chopped

3 garlic cloves, peeled and minced

2 teaspoons grated lime zest

Salt and freshly ground black pepper to taste

¼ cup olive oil

Margarita Marinade

Yield: ¾ cup | Active time: 10 minutes | Start to finish: 10 minutes | Uses: Chicken, fish and seafood

Combine lime juice, tequila, triple sec, chile, garlic, lime zest, chili powder, cumin, sugar, salt, and pepper in a heavy resealable plastic bag, and mix well. Add oil, and mix well again. Add food to be marinated, turning the bag to coat food evenly. Marinate food according to chart above.

Note: The marinade can be refrigerated for up to 3 days, tightly covered.

¼ cup freshly squeezed lime juice

3 tablespoons tequila

2 tablespoons triple sec

1 large jalapeño or serrano chile, seeds and ribs removed, and finely chopped

2 garlic cloves, peeled and minced

2 teaspoons grated lime zest

1 tablespoon chili powder

1 teaspoon ground cumin

1 teaspoon granulated sugar

Salt and freshly ground black pepper to taste

¼ cup vegetable oil

Beer Marinade

Yield: 1 cup | Active time: 5 minutes | Start to finish: 5 minutes | Uses: Chicken, fish and seafood

Combine beer, lemon juice, Worcestershire sauce, garlic, thyme, salt, and pepper sauce in a heavy resealable plastic bag, and mix well. Add oil, and mix well again. Add food to be marinated, turning the bag to coat food evenly. Marinate food according to chart above.

Note: The marinade can be refrigerated for up to 3 days, tightly covered.

¾ cup lager beer

3 tablespoons freshly squeezed lemon juice

1 tablespoon Worcestershire sauce

3 garlic cloves, peeled and minced

1 tablespoon fresh thyme or 1 teaspoon dried

Salt and hot red pepper sauce to taste

3 tablespoons olive oil

½ cup dry red wine

2 tablespoons balsamic vinegar

2 tablespoons gin

2 tablespoons firmly packed dark brown sugar

2 tablespoons chopped fresh thyme or 2 teaspoons dried

2 tablespoons chopped fresh rosemary or 2 teaspoons dried

3 garlic cloves, peeled and minced

2 teaspoons grated orange zest

1 teaspoon grated lemon zest

2 bay leaves, crumbled

¼ teaspoon ground cloves

Salt and freshly ground black pepper to taste

¼ cup olive oil

Hearty Red Wine Marinade

Yield: 1 cup | Active time: 10 minutes | Start to finish: 10 minutes | Uses: Beef, lamb, venison

Combine wine, vinegar, gin, brown sugar, thyme, rosemary, garlic, orange zest, lemon zest, bay leaves, cloves, salt, and pepper in a heavy resealable plastic bag, and mix well. Add oil, and mix well again. Add food to be marinated, turning the bag to coat food evenly. Marinate food according to chart above.

Note: The marinade can be refrigerated for up to 3 days, tightly covered.

¼ cup mirin or plum wine*

2 tablespoons soy sauce

2 tablespoons orange juice concentrate, thawed

4 garlic cloves, peeled and minced

1 tablespoon Chinese chile paste with garlic*

2 teaspoons grated orange zest

2 tablespoons vegetable oil

2 tablespoons Asian sesame oil*

* Available in the Asian aisle of most supermarkets and in specialty markets.

Spicy Asian Orange Marinade

Yield: ¾ cup | Active time: 5 minutes | Start to finish: 5 minutes | Uses: Pork, chicken, fish and seafood

Combine mirin, soy sauce, orange juice concentrate, garlic, chile paste, and orange zest in a heavy resealable plastic bag, and mix well. Add vegetable oil and sesame oil, and mix well again. Add food to be marinated, turning the bag to coat food evenly. Marinate food according to chart above.

Note: The marinade can be refrigerated for up to 3 days, tightly covered.

South American Marinade

Yield: 1 cup | Active time: 10 minutes | Start to finish: 10 minutes | Uses: Chicken, fish and seafood

Combine wine, lemon juice, onion, garlic, parsley, thyme, oregano, salt, and pepper in a heavy resealable plastic bag, and mix well. Add oil, and mix well again. Add food to be marinated, turning the bag to coat food evenly. Marinate food according to chart above.

Note: The marinade can be refrigerated for up to 3 days, tightly covered.

¼ cup dry white wine

1 tablespoon freshly squeezed lemon juice

1 small onion, peeled and finely chopped

2 garlic cloves, peeled and minced

¼ cup chopped fresh parsley

1 tablespoon fresh thyme or 1 teaspoon dried

1 tablespoon chopped fresh oregano or 1 teaspoon dried

Salt and freshly ground black pepper to taste

⅓ cup olive oil

Brines

Brining, along with smoking and salting, is the way that food was preserved prior to refrigeration and freezing. It is making a comeback today because the long soaking in flavored salty-sweet water improves the flavor and texture of foods, especially lean foods such as poultry and pork. Food such as thin pork chops can be brined for as little as 8 hours, while whole chickens or thick pork loins should be brined for at least 48 hours.

Chile Brine

Yield: 2 quarts | Active time: 10 minutes | Start to finish: 15 minutes | Uses: Pork, chicken, turkey

1. Combine salt, honey, vinegar, chiles, red pepper flakes, and 1 cup water in a large nonreactive saucepan, and stir well. Bring to a boil over medium-high heat, stirring occasionally. Reduce the heat to low and simmer 2 minutes.

2. Add remaining water to the pan, and allow brine to cool. Transfer brine to a large container, and add food to be brined. Cover and refrigerate.

1 cup kosher salt

1½ cups honey

½ cup cider vinegar

2 jalapeño or serrano chiles, halved

1 tablespoon crushed red pepper flakes

6 cups cold water

Apple Cider Brine

Yield: 2 quarts | Active time: 10 minutes | Start to finish: 15 minutes | Uses: Pork, chicken, turkey

1. Combine salt, sugar, apple juice concentrate, cloves, nutmeg, cinnamon, and 1 cup water in a large nonreactive saucepan, and stir well. Bring to a boil over medium-high heat, stirring occasionally. Reduce the heat to low and simmer 2 minutes.

2. Add remaining water to the pan, and allow brine to cool. Transfer brine to a large container, and add food to be brined. Cover and refrigerate.

1 cup kosher salt

½ cup granulated sugar

1 (6-ounce) can apple juice concentrate, thawed

2 tablespoons whole cloves

3 whole nutmeg, crushed

4 cinnamon sticks, crushed

7 cups cold water

1 cup kosher salt

1 cup firmly packed dark
  brown sugar

¼ cup chopped fresh thyme
  or 2 tablespoons dried

¼ cup chopped fresh sage
  or 2 tablespoons dried

3 tablespoons black
  peppercorns

2 quarts cold water

Brown Sugar Brine

Yield: 2 quarts | Active time: 5 minutes | Start to finish: 10 minutes | Uses: Pork, chicken, turkey

1. Combine salt, brown sugar, thyme, sage, peppercorns, and 1 cup water in a large nonreactive saucepan, and stir well. Bring to a boil over medium-high heat, stirring occasionally. Reduce the heat to low and simmer 2 minutes.

2. Add remaining water to the pan, and allow brine to cool. Transfer brine to a large container, and add food to be brined. Cover and refrigerate.

Chapter 3

Sauces for Basting and Topping

There are chapters later in this book devoted to specific dishes, many of which have sauces to top the food after it comes off the grill. The recipes in this chapter are for sauces that can be served successfully on a wide variety of foods that are grilled without one of the flavoring methods detailed in Chapter 2. The foods are simple so the sauces make them special.

Tomatillo Sauce

1 cup mayonnaise

⅔ cup sour cream

3 tablespoons freshly squeezed lime juice

3 scallions, white parts and 2 inches of green tops, rinsed, trimmed, and chopped

3 garlic cloves, peeled and minced

3 chipotle chiles in adobo sauce, finely chopped

1 teaspoon adobo sauce

Salt and freshly ground black pepper to taste

Creamy Chipotle Sauce

Yield: 2 cups | Active time: 10 minutes | Start to finish: 10 minutes | Uses: Poultry, fish and seafood, vegetables

Combine mayonnaise, sour cream, lime juice, scallions, garlic, chipotle chiles, and adobo sauce in a mixing bowl. Whisk well, and season to taste with salt and pepper.

Note: The sauce can be made up to 3 days in advance and refrigerated, tightly covered.

---

3 tablespoons olive oil

1 small onion, peeled and finely chopped

3 garlic cloves, peeled and minced

2 tablespoons chili powder

1 tablespoon ground cumin

¾ cup chicken stock or vegetable stock

1 (15-ounce) can tomato sauce

1 (4-ounce) can chopped mild green chiles, drained

¼ cup chopped fresh cilantro

Salt and freshly ground black pepper to taste

Tex-Mex Tomato Sauce

Yield: 2 cups | Active time: 15 minutes | Start to finish: 35 minutes | Uses: Meats, poultry, fish and seafood, vegetables

1. Heat olive oil in a 2-quart heavy saucepan over medium-high heat. Add onion and garlic and cook, stirring frequently, for 3 minutes, or until onion is translucent. Reduce the heat to low, stir in chili powder and cumin, and cook, stirring constantly, for 1 minute.

2. Stir in stock, tomato sauce, and green chiles. Whisk well, bring to a boil, and simmer sauce, uncovered, for 15 minutes, stirring occasionally, or until the sauce is reduced by one-quarter.

3. Stir in cilantro, and season to taste with salt and pepper. Serve hot or at room temperature.

Note: The sauce can be made up to 3 days in advance and refrigerated, tightly covered. Bring it back to room temperature or to a simmer before serving.

---

2 tablespoons olive oil

2 shallots, peeled and chopped

2 garlic cloves, peeled and minced

2 tablespoons chili powder

2 teaspoons ground cumin

⅔ cup ketchup

2 tablespoons prepared horseradish

2 tablespoons honey

1 tablespoon Dijon mustard

Salt and freshly ground pepper to taste

Southwestern Chile Sauce

Yield: 1½ cups | Active time: 15 minutes | Start to finish: 15 minutes | Uses: Meats and poultry

1. Heat olive oil in a small saucepan over medium-high heat. Add shallots and garlic and cook, stirring frequently, for 3 minutes, or until shallots are translucent. Stir in chili powder and cumin, and cook, stirring constantly, for 1 minute.

2. Stir in ketchup, horseradish, honey, and mustard, and bring to a boil over medium heat, stirring frequently. Reduce the heat to low, and simmer sauce for 5 minutes. Season to taste with salt and pepper, and keep warm.

Note: The sauce can be made up to 3 days in advance and refrigerated, tightly covered. Reheat it over low heat, stirring occasionally.

Quick Green Chile Sauce

Yield: 2 cups | Active time: 10 minutes | Start to finish: 25 minutes | Uses: Meats, poultry, fish and seafood, vegetables

1. Heat olive oil in a 2-quart heavy saucepan over medium-high heat. Add onion and garlic and cook, stirring frequently, for 3 minutes, or until onion is translucent. Reduce the heat to low, stir in cumin, and cook, stirring constantly, for 1 minute.

2. Stir in chiles and stock. Whisk well, bring to a boil, and simmer, uncovered, for 15 minutes, stirring occasionally, or until reduced by one-quarter. Combine cold water and cornstarch in a small bowl, and stir to dissolve cornstarch. Add to sauce, and bring to a simmer, stirring constantly. Cook over low heat for 1–2 minutes, or until sauce thickens.

3. Stir in cilantro, and season to taste with salt and pepper. Serve hot or at room temperature.

Note: The sauce can be made up to 3 days in advance and refrigerated, tightly covered. Bring it back to room temperature or to a simmer before serving.

2 tablespoons olive oil

½ small red onion, peeled and finely chopped

2 garlic cloves, peeled and minced

2 tablespoons ground cumin

3 (4-ounce) cans chopped mild green chiles, drained

1 cup chicken stock or vegetable stock

1 tablespoon cold water

2 teaspoons cornstarch

3 tablespoons chopped fresh cilantro

Salt and freshly ground black pepper to taste

Salsa Verde

Yield: 1½ cups | Active time: 15 minutes | Start to finish: 25 minutes | Uses: Fish and seafood, poultry

1. Combine tomatoes, tomatillo, and chicken stock in a small saucepan, and bring to a boil over medium heat. Simmer for 5 minutes, or until tomatoes are soft. Scrape mixture into a food processor fitted with a steel blade or into a blender.

2. Heat oil in a small skillet over medium-high heat. Add chile and garlic, and cook, stirring frequently, for 2 minutes. Add to food processor or blender, along with cilantro.

3. Chop finely using on-and-off pulsing; do not puree mixture. Scrape mixture into a bowl, and season to taste with salt and pepper. Keep warm.

Note: The sauce can be prepared up to 2 days in advance and refrigerated, tightly covered. Reheat it over low heat, but do not allow it to boil.

½ pound green tomatoes, rinsed, cored, and diced

1 medium tomatillo, husk discarded, rinsed, cored, and diced

½ cup chicken stock

2 tablespoons olive oil

1 jalapeño or serrano chile, seeds and ribs removed, and finely chopped

2 garlic cloves, peeled and minced

2 tablespoons chopped fresh cilantro

Salt and freshly ground black pepper to taste

3 pounds fresh tomatillos

3 garlic cloves, peeled

2–3 serrano or jalapeño chiles, stemmed, seeds and ribs removed

2 tablespoons olive oil

2 teaspoons granulated sugar

¾ cup chicken stock

¼ cup chopped fresh cilantro

Salt and freshly ground black pepper to taste

Tomatillo Sauce

Yield: 3 cups | Active time: 15 minutes | Start to finish: 25 minutes | Uses: Poultry, fish and seafood

1. Discard husks from tomatillos, and rinse well. Core and dice tomatillos.

2. Combine tomatillos, chiles, and garlic in a food processor fitted with a steel blade or in a blender. Puree until smooth.

3. Heat olive oil in a 2-quart saucepan over medium-high heat. Add puree, and cook for 2 minutes. Add sugar and stock, bring to a boil, and reduce the heat to low. Simmer sauce 10 minutes, stirring occasionally.

4. Stir in cilantro, and season to taste with salt and pepper. Keep warm.

Note: The sauce can be refrigerated for up to 3 days, tightly covered, or it can be frozen for up to 3 months. If freezing the sauce, add cilantro when reheating it.

1 (20-ounce) bottle ketchup

1 cup cider vinegar

½ cup firmly packed dark brown sugar

5 tablespoons Worcestershire sauce

¼ cup vegetable oil

2 tablespoons dry mustard

2 garlic cloves, peeled and minced

1 tablespoon grated fresh ginger

1 lemon, thinly sliced

½–1 teaspoon hot red pepper sauce, or to taste

My Favorite Barbecue Sauce

Yield: 4 cups | Active time: 10 minutes | Start to finish: 40 minutes | Uses: Meats, poultry

1. Combine ketchup, vinegar, brown sugar, Worcestershire sauce, vegetable oil, mustard, garlic, ginger, lemon, and red pepper sauce in a heavy 2-quart sauce-pan, and bring to a boil over medium heat, stirring occasionally.

2. Reduce the heat to low and simmer sauce, uncovered, for 30 minutes, or until thick, stirring occasionally. Strain sauce, pressing with the back of a spoon to extract as much liquid as possible. Ladle sauce into containers and refrigerate, tightly covered.

Note: The sauce can be made up to 1 week in advance and refrigerated, tightly covered. Bring it back to room temperature before serving.

Southwestern Barbecue Sauce

Yield: 3 cups | Active time: 15 minutes | Start to finish: 25 minutes | Uses: Meats, poultry

1. Heat oil in a saucepan over medium-high heat. Add onion, garlic, and chiles and cook, stirring frequently, for 5 minutes, or until onion softens. Stir in tomatoes, sugar, vinegar, lime juice, and mustard, and bring to a boil over medium heat, stirring frequently.

2. Reduce the heat to low and simmer sauce, uncovered, for 15 minutes. Season to taste with salt and red pepper sauce, and keep warm.

Note: The sauce can be made up to 1 week in advance and refrigerated, tightly covered. Bring it back to room temperature before serving.

2 tablespoons olive oil

1 large onion, peeled and chopped

2 garlic cloves, peeled and minced

2 canned chipotle chiles in adobo sauce, drained and finely chopped

2 cups crushed tomatoes in tomato puree

½ cup firmly packed dark brown sugar

¼ cup cider vinegar

3 tablespoons freshly squeezed lime juice

2 teaspoons dry mustard

Salt and hot red pepper sauce to taste

Southwestern Barbecue Sauce

¼ cup olive oil

1 medium onion, peeled and finely chopped

4 garlic cloves, peeled and minced

1 carrot, peeled and finely chopped

1 celery rib, rinsed, trimmed, and finely chopped

1 (28-ounce) can crushed tomatoes

2 tablespoons chopped fresh parsley

2 tablespoons chopped fresh oregano or 2 teaspoons dried

1 tablespoon fresh thyme or 1 teaspoon dried

2 bay leaves

Salt and crushed red pepper flakes to taste

Herbed Tomato Sauce

Yield: 2 cups | Active time: 15 minutes | Start to finish: 1 hour | Uses: Meats, poultry, fish and seafood, vegetables

1. Heat olive oil in 2-quart saucepan over medium heat. Add onion and garlic and cook, stirring frequently, for 3 minutes, or until onion is translucent.

2. Add carrot, celery, tomatoes, parsley, oregano, thyme, and bay leaves. Bring to a boil, reduce heat to low, and simmer sauce, uncovered, stirring occasionally, for 40 minutes, or until slightly thickened. Season to taste with salt and red pepper flakes and discard bay leaves.

Note: The sauce can be made up to 3 days in advance and refrigerated, tightly covered. Bring back to a simmer before serving. It can also be frozen for up to 3 months.

½ pound mild feta cheese, diced

½ cup sour cream

¼ cup plain whole-milk yogurt, preferably Greek

¼ cup extra-virgin olive oil

2 tablespoons freshly squeezed lemon juice

2 garlic cloves, peeled

¼ cup chopped fresh dill or 2 tablespoons dried

Salt and freshly ground black pepper to taste

Greek Feta Sauce

Yield: 1½ cups | Active time: 10 minutes | Start to finish: 10 minutes | Uses: Fish and seafood, poultry, vegetables

1. Combine feta, sour cream, yogurt, olive oil, lemon juice, and garlic in a food processor fitted with a steel blade or in a blender. Puree until smooth. Scrape mixture into a mixing bowl, and stir in dill. Season to taste with salt and pepper, and refrigerate sauce until ready to use.

Note: The sauce can be made up to 3 days in advance and refrigerated, tightly covered. Bring it back to room temperature before serving.

Instant Asian Barbecue Sauce

Yield: 2 cups | Active time: 10 minutes | Start to finish: 10 minutes | Uses: Poultry, fish and seafood, vegetables

Combine applesauce, hoisin sauce, brown sugar, ketchup, honey, rice vinegar, soy sauce, and chile paste in a mixing bowl. Whisk until smooth. Refrigerate until ready to use.

Note: The sauce can be made up to 3 days in advance and refrigerated, tightly covered.

¾ cup unsweetened applesauce

½ cup hoisin sauce*

¼ cup firmly packed dark brown sugar

6 tablespoons ketchup

2 tablespoons honey

2 tablespoons rice vinegar

1 tablespoon soy sauce

1 tablespoon Chinese chile paste with garlic*, or to taste (or hot red pepper sauce can be substituted)

* Available in the Asian aisle of most supermarkets and in specialty markets.

Spicy Thai Peanut Sauce

Yield: 2 cups | Active time: 10 minutes | Start to finish: 30 minutes, including 20 minutes for chilling | Uses: Meats, poultry, fish and seafood, vegetables

Combine peanut butter, water, brown sugar, lime juice, soy sauce, sesame oil, and chile paste in a mixing bowl. Whisk until well combined. Stir in garlic, scallions, and cilantro, and chill well before serving.

Note: The sauce can be made up to 3 days in advance and refrigerated, tightly covered. Bring it back to room temperature before serving.

1 cup chunky peanut butter

½ cup very hot tap water

½ cup firmly packed dark brown sugar

⅓ cup freshly squeezed lime juice

¼ cup soy sauce

2 tablespoons Asian sesame oil*

2 tablespoons Chinese chile paste with garlic*

6 garlic cloves, peeled and minced

3 scallions, rinsed, trimmed, and chopped

¼ cup chopped fresh cilantro

* Available in the Asian aisle of most supermarkets and in specialty markets.

Dilled Cucumber Raita

Yield: 2 cups | Active time: 10 minutes | Start to finish: 10 minutes | Uses: Meats, poultry, fish and seafood

½ medium cucumber, peeled, seeded, and finely chopped

2 ripe plum tomatoes, cored, seeded, and finely chopped

2 scallions, white parts and 3 inches of green tops, rinsed, trimmed, and finely chopped

2 garlic cloves, peeled and minced

1 cup plain whole-milk yogurt

2 tablespoons chopped fresh dill or 2 teaspoons dried

2 tablespoons freshly squeezed lemon juice

Salt and freshly ground black pepper to taste

Combine cucumber, tomatoes, scallions, garlic, yogurt, dill, and lemon juice in a mixing bowl. Stir well, and season to taste with salt and pepper. Refrigerate until ready to use.

Note: The sauce can be made up to 3 days in advance and refrigerated, tightly covered.

Hazelnut Vinaigrette

Yield: 2 cups | Active time: 10 minutes | Start to finish: 20 minutes | Uses: Poultry, fish and seafood, vegetables

1 cup hazelnuts

3 tablespoons sherry vinegar

3 tablespoons Madeira

1 tablespoon Dijon mustard

1 teaspoon granulated sugar

Salt and freshly ground black pepper to taste

1 cup hazelnut oil

1. Preheat the oven to 350°F. Place hazelnuts on a baking sheet and toast them for 6 to 8 minutes, or until they are lightly browned. Let cool and transfer to a food processor fitted with a steel blade. Chop hazelnuts finely, using on-and-off pulsing. Set aside.

2. Combine vinegar, Madeira, mustard, sugar, salt, and pepper in a jar with a tight-fitting lid, and shake well. Add hazelnut oil and hazelnuts, and shake well again.

Note: The dressing can be made up to 3 days in advance and refrigerated, tightly covered. Bring it back to room temperature before using.

Chapter 4

Hors d'Oeuvres and Appetizers

When you have the grill lit for the main course of a meal, it only makes sense to utilize this versatile cooking tool for more than one dish. In this chapter you will find recipes for small nibbles to enjoy with a cocktail or glass of wine before dinner, as well as small first courses—most of them seafood—to serve at the table. Many of the recipes in this chapter are excellent for buffet entertaining and cocktail parties too. In addition to the dishes in this chapter, also take a look at the soups and salads in Chapter 5 for other light options to begin a meal.

Southwest Chicken Pinwheels

Yield: 24 pieces | Active time: 20 minutes | Start to finish: 1½ hours, including 1 hour for chilling

1. Prepare a hot grill according to the instructions given in Chapter 1.

2. Trim chicken breasts of all visible fat, and pound to an even thickness of ½ inch between two sheets of plastic wrap. Combine olive oil, garlic, chili powder, salt, and pepper in a small bowl, and stir well. Rub mixture on both sides of chicken.

3. Drain salsa in a strainer, pressing to extract as much liquid as possible. Combine salsa, cream cheese, and cilantro in a mixing bowl and stir well. Set aside.

4. Grill chicken for 2–3 minutes per side, uncovered, or until chicken is cooked through and no longer pink. Cut chicken crosswise into thin strips.

5. Wrap tortillas in plastic wrap and microwave on high (100%) for 20–30 seconds, or until soft and pliable. Place tortillas on a counter, and spread each with cream cheese mixture. Arrange chicken slices on the bottom half of each tortilla. Place ½ cup mesclun at the bottom edge of tortilla on top of chicken. Roll tortillas firmly but gently, starting at the filled edge. Place rolls, seam-side down, on a platter or ungreased baking sheet, and refrigerate for 1 hour.

6. Trim end off each roll by cutting on the diagonal to remove portion of tortilla that does not meet and form a log. Slice each tortilla into 6 slices and serve chilled.

Note: The tortillas can be filled up to 6 hours in advance and refrigerated, tightly covered. Slice just before serving.

Ingredients (sidebar):

- 2 (6-ounce) boneless skinless chicken breast halves
- 2 tablespoons olive oil
- 2 garlic cloves, peeled and minced
- 1 tablespoon chili powder
- Salt and freshly ground black pepper to taste
- 1 cup Summer Tomato Salsa (recipe on page 102) or good-quality refrigerated salsa (do not use bottled salsa)
- 1 (3-ounce) package cream cheese, softened
- ¼ cup chopped fresh cilantro
- 4 (8-inch) flour tortillas
- 2 cups mesclun salad mix or other baby greens, rinsed and dried

1 small red onion, peeled and halved lengthwise

¼ cup olive oil, divided

24 slices French or Italian bread, ½ inch thick

3 garlic cloves, peeled

5 ripe plum tomatoes, cored, seeded, and finely chopped

¼ cup crumbled feta cheese

¼ cup chopped black olives

2 tablespoons chopped mild green chiles, drained

1 teaspoon smoked Spanish paprika

½ teaspoon ground cumin

Salt and freshly ground black pepper to taste

Tomato and Olive Bruschetta

Yield: 24 pieces | Active time: 20 minutes | Start to finish: 50 minutes

1. Prepare a medium-hot grill according to the instructions given in Chapter 1.

2. Brush onion with olive oil. Grill onion, turning with tongs occasionally, for 12–15 minutes, or until onion is tender. Remove onion halves from the grill, and allow them to cool.

3. While onion grills, brush bread slices with oil, and grill for 2 minutes per side, or until toasted. Cut 1 garlic clove in half, and rub on 1 side of toast. Set aside.

4. Discarding root end, chop onion. Mince remaining 2 garlic cloves. Combine onion, garlic, tomatoes, feta, olives, chiles, paprika, cumin, and remaining olive oil in a mixing bowl. Season to taste with salt and pepper.

5. To serve, mound topping on toast slices, and serve immediately.

Note: The topping and the toast slices can be prepared up to 3 hours in advance and kept at room temperature.

Tomato and Olive Bruschetta

Southwestern Poblano Bruschetta

Yield: 24 pieces | Active time: 20 minutes | Start to finish: 50 minutes

1. Prepare a medium-hot grill according to the instructions given in Chapter 1.

2. Grill peppers on all sides until skin is charred and black, turning them gently with tongs. Remove peppers from the grill, and place them in a heavy plastic bag; allow them to stand for 10 minutes.

3. While peppers are grilling, brush bread slices with oil, and grill for 2 minutes per side, or until toasted. Cut 1 garlic clove in half, and rub on 1 side of toast. Set aside.

4. Remove skin and seeds from peppers, and chop peppers finely. Mince 2 remaining garlic cloves. Combine peppers, garlic, oregano, lemon juice, and remaining olive oil in a mixing bowl. Season to taste with salt and pepper.

5. To serve, mound topping on toast slices, and serve immediately.

Note: The topping and the toast slices can be prepared up to 3 hours in advance and kept at room temperature.

4 large poblano peppers

24 slices French or Italian bread, ½ inch thick

¼ cup extra-virgin olive oil, divided

3 garlic cloves, peeled

3 tablespoons chopped fresh oregano or 1 tablespoon dried

1 tablespoon freshly squeezed lemon juice

Salt and freshly ground black pepper to taste

Grilled Corn and Sausage Salad

Yield: 6–8 servings | Active time: 15 minutes | Start to finish: 1 hour

1. Prepare a medium-hot grill according to the instructions given in Chapter 1. If using a charcoal grill, soak mesquite chips in water for 30 minutes. If using a gas grill, create a packet for wood chips as described in Chapter 1.

2. Remove all but one layer of husks from corn and pull out the corn silks. Soak corn in cold water to cover for 10 minutes. Place wood chips on the grill. Grill corn, covered, for 10–15 minutes, turning with tongs occasionally.

3. When corn is cool enough to handle, discard husks, and cut kernels off cobs using a sharp serrated knife.

4. Cook sausage in a frying pan over medium heat, breaking up lumps with a fork. Cook until brown. Combine sausage and its fat with corn, red and green bell peppers, and scallions in a mixing bowl.

5. Combine olive oil, lime juice, maple syrup, salt, and pepper in a jar with a tight-fitting lid. Shake well, and toss with the corn mixture. Toss with cilantro, and serve at room temperature on top of lettuce leaves.

Note: The salad can be made up to 2 days in advance and refrigerated, tightly covered with plastic wrap. Allow it to sit at room temperature for a few hours to take the chill off. Do not add the cilantro until just before serving.

1 cup mesquite chips

4 ears fresh corn, unshucked

¾ pound bulk pork sausage

½ cup finely chopped red bell pepper

½ cup finely chopped green bell pepper

3 scallions, white parts and 2 inches of the green tops, trimmed and finely chopped

3 tablespoons olive oil

2 tablespoons freshly squeezed lime juice

2 tablespoons pure maple syrup

Salt and freshly ground black pepper to taste

3 tablespoons finely chopped cilantro

6–8 leaves romaine, rinsed and dried

4 boneless and skinless chicken breast halves

½ cup soy sauce

½ cup firmly packed dark brown sugar

¼ cup freshly squeezed lime juice

2 tablespoons Chinese chile paste with garlic*

4 garlic cloves, peeled and minced

1 tablespoon Asian sesame oil*

1 cup Spicy Thai Peanut Sauce (recipe on page 23)

* Available in the Asian aisle of most supermarkets and in specialty markets.

Chicken Satay

Yield: 36 pieces | Active time: 15 minutes | Start to finish: 3¼ hours, including 3 hours for marinating

1. Trim fat from chicken breasts and pull off tenderloins. Remove tendon from the center of each tenderloin by holding down tip with your finger and scraping away meat with the dull side of a paring knife. Cut tenderloins in half, and cut the remaining chicken meat into 1-inch cubes.

2. Combine soy sauce, brown sugar, lime juice, chile paste, garlic, and sesame oil in a heavy resealable plastic bag, and blend well. Add chicken pieces and marinate, refrigerated, for 3 hours, turning the bag occasionally.

3. Prepare a medium-hot grill according to the instructions given in Chapter 1.

4. Remove chicken from marinade and discard marinade. Grill chicken pieces, uncovered if using a charcoal grill, turning pieces with tongs, for a total of 3–5 minutes or until brown and cooked through. Spear each piece of chicken with a toothpick or bamboo skewer and serve hot with a cup of Spicy Thai Peanut Sauce for dipping.

VARIATION: *Cubes of pork or beef, large shrimp, or strips of salmon can become satay as well as chicken.*

Note: The chicken can marinate for up to 6 hours, and it can be cooked 1 day in advance and refrigerated, tightly covered. Reheat it wrapped in aluminum foil in a 350°F oven for 5–10 minutes, or until hot.

Chicken Satay

Southwestern Marinated Sea Scallops

Yield: 6–8 servings | Active time: 30 minutes | Start to finish: 2 hours, including 45 minutes for marinating

1. Prepare a hot grill according to the instructions given in Chapter 1.

2. Toss scallops with 2 tablespoons oil, and season to taste with salt and pepper. Cut peel (including all white pith) from orange using a small serrated knife. Dice orange, and set aside.

3. Grill scallops, uncovered if using a charcoal grill, turning once, until just cooked through, about 5 minutes. Remove scallops from the grill, and allow them to cool. Cut scallops into quarters.

4. Combine scallops, orange, lime juice, cucumber, onion, chile, and remaining oil in a mixing bowl. Season to taste with salt and pepper, and refrigerate scallops, covered, for at least 45 minutes, or until cold.

5. Stir cilantro into scallop mixture. To serve, divide salad greens onto individual plates, and mound scallop mixture in the center.

VARIATION: *Large shrimp or 1-inch cubes of any firm-fleshed white fish, such as cod or halibut, can be used in place of scallops.*

Note: The scallops can be cooked and the mixture can be prepared up to 1 day in advance and refrigerated separately, tightly covered. Do not mix scallops into vegetable mixture more than 2 hours in advance.

2 pounds large sea scallops, rinsed and patted dry with paper towels

¼ cup olive oil, divided

Salt and freshly ground black pepper to taste

1 navel orange

¼ cup freshly squeezed lime juice

½ English cucumber, cut into 1/3-inch dice

¼ small red onion, peeled and chopped

1 small jalapeño or serrano chile, seeds and ribs removed, and finely chopped

¼ cup chopped fresh cilantro

3–4 cups mixed salad greens, rinsed and dried

24 large oysters in their shells

¼ cup pine nuts

2 garlic cloves, peeled

2 jalapeño or serrano chiles, seeds and ribs removed

1½ cups firmly packed fresh cilantro leaves

¼ cup olive oil

¼ cup freshly grated Parmesan cheese

Salt and freshly ground black pepper to taste

Oysters with Cilantro Pesto

Yield: 4–6 servings | Active time: 15 minutes | Start to finish: 40 minutes

1. Prepare a medium-hot grill according to the instructions given in Chapter 1. Preheat the oven to 350°F. Scrub oysters well under cold running water. Discard any that do not shut tightly while being scrubbed.

2. Toast pine nuts on a baking sheet for 5–7 minutes, or until lightly browned. Combine pine nuts, garlic, chiles, cilantro, olive oil, and Parmesan cheese in a food processor fitted with a steel blade or in a blender. Puree until smooth, and season to taste with salt and pepper. Set aside.

3. Place oysters on the grill with rounded side down. Grill, covered, 3–4 minutes. Remove oysters with tongs, and place on a hot pad. Remove and discard top shell with an oyster knife, being careful not to spill oyster liquor. Separate oysters from bottom shell, but do not remove oysters.

4. Top each oyster with 1 tablespoon of pesto mixture. Return oysters to grill, and grill, covered, for 2–3 minutes more, or until edges of oysters curl. Serve immediately.

VARIATION: *Large littleneck clams can be substituted for the oysters.*

Note: The pesto mixture can be prepared up to 3 days in advance and refrigerated, tightly covered with plastic wrap. Allow pesto to reach room temperature before using.

Grilled Oysters

Grilled Oysters

Yield: 4–6 servings | Active time: 15 minutes | Start to finish: 40 minutes

1. Prepare a medium-hot grill according to the instructions given in Chapter 1. Scrub oysters well under cold running water. Discard any that do not shut tightly while being scrubbed.

2. Combine butter, garlic, parsley, chives, salt, and pepper in a small bowl, and beat until smooth.

3. Place oysters on the grill with rounded side down. Grill, covered, 3–4 minutes. Remove oysters with tongs, and place on a hot pad. Remove and discard top shell with an oyster knife, being careful not to spill oyster liquor. Separate oysters from bottom shell, but do not remove oyster.

4. Top each oyster with 2 teaspoons seasoned butter. Return oysters to grill, and grill, covered, for 2–3 minutes more, or until edges of oysters curl. Serve immediately.

VARIATION: *Large littleneck clams can be substituted for the oysters.*

Note: The butter mixture can be prepared up to 3 days in advance and refrigerated, tightly covered with plastic wrap. Allow butter to reach room temperature before using.

2 dozen oysters

4 tablespoons unsalted butter, softened

2 garlic cloves, peeled and minced

3 tablespoons chopped fresh parsley

2 tablespoons chopped fresh chives

Salt and freshly ground black pepper to taste

Chapter 5:

Soups and Small Vegetable Salads

Hot soups to warm you in winter or chilly soups to cool you in summer are always a welcome way to begin a meal, or a satisfying focus of a light supper or lunch. Most of the recipes in this chapter include component parts that spend some time cooking on the grill, so their aroma and flavor permeates the broth.

Small vegetable salads are another starter as versatile as they are delicious (for grilled salad entrees, see Chapter 11). All of the salad recipes in this chapter can become part of a buffet dinner.

4 (6-inch) corn tortillas

3 ears fresh corn, shucked

¼ cup olive oil, divided

Salt and freshly ground black pepper to taste

1 medium onion, peeled and chopped

2 garlic cloves, peeled and minced

1 large jalapeño or serrano chile, seeds and ribs removed, and finely chopped

2 teaspoons dried oregano

2 teaspoons dried cumin

6 cups chicken stock

1 (14.5-ounce) can diced tomatoes, drained

1 lime, cut into wedges

⅓ cup chopped fresh cilantro

1 ripe avocado, peeled and diced

1 cup grated Monterey Jack cheese

Tex-Mex Tortilla Soup

Yield: 4–6 servings | Active time: 20 minutes | Start to finish: 55 minutes

1. Prepare a medium-hot grill according to the instructions given in Chapter 1.

2. Brush tortillas and corn with 2 tablespoons oil, and sprinkle with salt and pepper. Grill tortillas for 1 minute per side, or until crisp. Remove tortillas from the grill, and break into 1-inch pieces.

3. Grill corn, covered, for a total of 8–10 minutes, turning it every 2 minutes, or until kernels are browned. Remove corn from the grill, and when cool enough to handle, cut kernels from cobs using a sharp, serrated knife.

4. While corn grills, heat remaining oil in a heavy 2-quart saucepan over medium-high heat. Add onion, garlic, and chile, and cook, stirring frequently, for 3 minutes, or until onion is translucent. Stir in oregano and cumin, and cook for 1 minute, stirring constantly. Add chicken stock and tomatoes, and bring to a boil over medium-high heat.

5. Reduce the heat to low, and simmer soup, uncovered, for 15 minutes. Add corn, and simmer an additional 5 minutes. Season to taste with salt and pepper.

6. To serve, ladle soup into bowls, and top with tortilla pieces. Pass lime wedges, avocado, and cheese separately.

VARIATION: *Have some leftover grilled chicken or fish around? Add it along with the corn kernels, and you will have a heartier soup.*

Note: The soup can be made up to 2 days in advance and refrigerated, tightly covered. Reheat soup slowly, but do not let it boil or reduce.

Farmers' Market Vegetable Soup

Yield: 4–6 servings | Active time: 20 minutes | Start to finish: 1 hour

1. Prepare a medium-hot grill according to the instructions given in Chapter 1.

2. Brush eggplant, zucchini, yellow squash, onion, and bell pepper slices with olive oil, reserving 1 tablespoon. Sprinkle vegetables with salt and pepper.

3. Grill vegetables, covered, for a total of 8 minutes, turning them once. Remove vegetables from the grill. Peel pepper, and then cut all vegetables into a ½-inch dice.

4. Heat remaining oil in a heavy 2-quart saucepan over medium-high heat. Add garlic, and cook, stirring constantly, for 1 minute. Add stock, tomatoes, parsley, oregano, and diced vegetables, and bring to a boil. Reduce the heat to low, and simmer soup, uncovered, for 15 minutes, stirring occasionally. Serve immediately.

Note: The soup can be made up to 2 days in advance and refrigerated, tightly covered. Reheat soup slowly, but do not let it boil or reduce.

- 1 Japanese eggplant, trimmed and cut lengthwise into ½-inch slices
- 1 zucchini, trimmed and cut lengthwise into ½-inch slices
- 1 yellow squash, trimmed and cut lengthwise into ½-inch slices
- 1 medium sweet onion, such as Vidalia or Bermuda, peeled and cut into ½-inch slices
- 1 large red bell pepper, seeds and ribs removed, and cut lengthwise into quarters
- ¼ cup olive oil, divided
- Salt and freshly ground black pepper to taste
- 2 garlic cloves, peeled and minced
- 4 cups chicken stock
- 1 (14.5-ounce) can diced tomatoes, drained
- ¼ cup chopped fresh parsley
- 2 tablespoons chopped fresh oregano or 2 teaspoons dried

Farmers' Market Vegetable Soup

1 medium Bermuda or other sweet white onion, peeled and quartered

1 medium cucumber, peeled, seeded, and cut into 1-inch sections

1 red bell pepper, seeds and ribs removed, and diced

3 medium to large ripe tomatoes, rinsed, seeded and diced,

3 large garlic cloves, peeled

1½ cups tomato juice

¼ cup extra-virgin olive oil

1 jalapeño or serrano chile, seeds and ribs removed

¼ cup balsamic vinegar

¼ cup chopped fresh cilantro

Salt and freshly ground black pepper to taste

For serving: 1 cup toasted croutons (optional)

Gazpacho

Yield: 6–8 servings | Active time: 20 minutes | Start to finish: 2 hours, including 1½ hours for chilling

1. Finely chop onion, cucumber, red pepper, and 1 tomato in a food processor fitted with a steel blade, using on-and-off pulsing. Scrape mixture into a large bowl.

2. Puree remaining tomatoes with garlic, tomato juice, olive oil, jalapeño, and balsamic vinegar. Stir puree into vegetables, add cilantro, and season to taste with salt and pepper. Chill for at least 1½ hours. Serve chilled, garnished with croutons, if using.

Note: The soup can be made up to 2 days in advance and refrigerated, tightly covered. Stir it well before serving

Gazpacho

Chilled Avocado Soup

Yield: 4–6 servings | Active time: 15 minutes | Start to finish: 1 hour, including 45 minutes for chilling

1. Combine avocados, onion, garlic, chiles, fresh chile, lime juice, chicken stock, sour cream, half-and-half, cilantro, salt, and cayenne in a food processor fitted with a steel blade or in a blender. Puree until smooth, and chill for at least 45 minutes.

2. To serve, sprinkle individual portions with chopped tomato and crushed tortilla chips.

Note: The soup can be made up to 1 day in advance and refrigerated, with plastic wrap pressed directly into the surface.

2 ripe avocados, peeled and diced

¼ medium onion, peeled and diced

1 garlic clove, peeled

1 (4-ounce) can diced green chiles, drained

1 small jalapeño or serrano chile, seeds and ribs removed

Juice of 1 lime

2 cups chicken stock, preferably homemade

½ cup sour cream

½ cup half-and-half

3 tablespoons chopped fresh cilantro

Salt and cayenne to taste

Chopped tomato and crushed tortilla chips

Grilled Corn Soup

Yield: 6–8 servings | Active time: 20 minutes | Start to finish: 1 hour

1. Prepare a medium-hot grill according to the instructions given in Chapter 1. If using a charcoal grill, soak mesquite chips in water for 30 minutes. If using a gas grill, create a packet for wood chips as described in Chapter 1.

2. Preheat the oven to 350°F. Bake garlic cloves for 15 minutes, and peel garlic when cool enough to handle. Set aside.

3. Remove all but one layer of husks from the corn, and pull out corn silks. Soak corn in cold water to cover for 10 minutes. Place mesquite chips on the grill. Grill corn, covered, for 10–15 minutes, turning with tongs occasionally. Remove corn from the grill, and when cool enough to handle, cut kernels from cobs using a sharp, serrated knife.

4. Melt butter in a large saucepan, and cook kernels over low heat for 5 minutes, stirring occasionally. Remove 1 cup of kernels, and set aside. Puree remaining corn, roasted garlic, cornmeal, chiles, and stock in a food processor fitted with a steel blade or in a blender. This will probably have to be done in a few batches.

5. Combine puree with milk and heat to a boil over medium heat. Add reserved corn kernels, and season to taste with salt and pepper. Reduce the heat to low, and simmer for 5 minutes, stirring occasionally.

Note: The soup can be made up to 2 days in advance and refrigerated, tightly covered. Reheat soup slowly, but do not let it boil or reduce. After it has been chilled, it may have to be thinned with a little additional milk or stock.

1 cup mesquite chips

4 large garlic cloves, unpeeled

8–10 medium ears fresh corn, unshucked

2 tablespoons unsalted butter

¼ cup yellow cornmeal

1 (4-ounce) can chopped mild green chiles, drained

2 cups chicken stock

2 cups milk

Salt and freshly ground black pepper to taste

⅓ cup red wine vinegar

¼ cup freshly squeezed orange juice

3 garlic cloves, peeled and minced, divided

2 teaspoons grated orange zest

Salt and freshly ground black pepper to taste

⅔ cup olive oil, divided

1 pound ripe tomatoes, rinsed, cored, and cut into ¾-inch dice

2 red, orange, or yellow bell peppers, seeds and ribs removed, and cut into 1-inch strips

1 pound zucchini, rinsed, trimmed, and cut on the diagonal into ⅓-inch slices

1 medium red onion, peeled and cut into ¼-inch slices

1 (12-ounce) loaf of hearty Italian bread, cut into 1-inch slices

¼ cup chopped fresh Italian parsley

Panzanella Salad

Yield: 4–6 servings | Active time: 20 minutes | Start to finish: 1 hour

1. Prepare a medium-hot grill according to the instructions given in Chapter 1.

2. Combine vinegar, orange juice, 2 garlic cloves, orange zest, salt, and pepper in a jar with a tight-fitting lid, and shake well. Add ½ cup olive oil, and shake well again. Set aside.

3. Place tomatoes in a large salad bowl, and sprinkle liberally with salt and pepper.

4. Brush pepper strips, zucchini, and onion with remaining olive oil. Rub bread slices with remaining minced garlic. Grill peppers and onion, covered, for a total of 4 minutes, and bread slices and zucchini for a total of 3 minutes, turning slices frequently, or until vegetables are tender and bread is toasted. Remove food from the grill.

5. Cut bread and vegetables into 1-inch pieces, and add to bowl with tomatoes. Toss with dressing, and allow to stand for 15 minutes. Serve immediately, sprinkled with parsley.

Note: The dressing can be prepared up to a day in advance and refrigerated; return to room temperature. Bread and vegetables can be grilled up to 4 hours in advance. Do not combine salad ingredients until 15 minutes before serving.

¼ cup freshly squeezed lemon juice

1 shallot, peeled and minced

2 garlic cloves, peeled and chopped

2 tablespoons chopped fresh marjoram or 2 teaspoons dried

Salt and freshly ground black pepper to taste

½ cup extra-virgin olive oil

4 ears fresh corn, shucked

1 (15-ounce) can pinto beans, drained and rinsed

1 pint cherry tomatoes, halved

¼ cup chopped fresh cilantro

Corn, Tomato, and Pinto Bean Salad

Yield: 4–6 servings | Active time: 25 minutes | Start to finish: 45 minutes

1. Prepare a medium-hot grill according to the instructions given in Chapter 1.

2. Combine lemon juice, shallot, garlic, marjoram, salt, and pepper in a jar with a tight-fitting lid, and shake well. Add olive oil, and shake well again. Set aside.

3. Grill corn, covered, for a total of 8 to 10 minutes, turning it every 2 minutes, or until kernels are browned. Remove corn from the grill, and when cool enough to handle, cut kernels from cobs using a sharp, serrated knife. Place corn in a large salad bowl.

4. Add pinto beans, tomatoes, and cilantro to the salad bowl. Toss salad with enough dressing to coat vegetables lightly.

5. To serve, divide vegetables on individual plates or arrange on a platter. Pass extra dressing separately.

Note: The dressing can be made up to 2 days in advance and refrigerated, tightly covered. Return to room temperature before dressing salad. Corn can be grilled up to 4 hours in advance and kept at room temperature.

Mixed Vegetable Salad with Oregano

Yield: 4–6 servings | Active time: 20 minutes | Start to finish: 45 minutes

1. Prepare a medium-hot grill according to the instructions given in Chapter 1.

2. Mix olive oil and garlic. Brush oil on both sides of eggplant, zucchini, yellow squash, and onion.

3. Grill all vegetables except tomatoes, covered, for a total of 10 minutes, turning occasionally, or until crisp-tender; add tomatoes for last 4 minutes of cooking time. Remove vegetables from the grill with tongs, and, when cool enough to handle, cut vegetables into 1-inch slices.

4. To serve, divide vegetables on individual plates or arrange on a platter. Season to taste with salt and pepper, then drizzle with vinegar and sprinkle with oregano.

Note: The vegetables can be grilled up to 4 hours in advance and kept at room temperature.

⅓ cup olive oil

2 garlic cloves, peeled and minced

2 Japanese eggplants, trimmed and quartered lengthwise

1 zucchini, trimmed and quartered lengthwise

1 yellow squash, trimmed and quartered lengthwise

1 small sweet onion, such as Vidalia or Bermuda, peeled and quartered

¼ pound mushrooms, wiped with a damp paper towel, and stemmed

6 ripe plum tomatoes, rinsed, halved, and seeded

Salt and freshly ground black pepper to taste

¼ cup balsamic vinegar

½ cup chopped fresh oregano

Mixed Vegetable Salad with Oregano

½ cup kosher salt

2 quarts cold water

2 (1-pound) eggplants, cut into ¾-inch-thick rounds

2 medium zucchini, quartered lengthwise

2 red bell peppers, seeds and ribs removed, and cut into 2-inch strips

1 large sweet onion, such as Vidalia or Bermuda, peeled and cut into ½-inch slices

½ pound large mushrooms, wiped clean with a damp paper towel, trimmed, and halved

⅓ cup olive oil

4 garlic cloves, peeled and minced

3 tablespoons herbes de Provence

Salt and freshly ground black pepper to taste

¼ cup balsamic vinegar

1 cup crumbled feta cheese

½ cup pitted oil-cured black olives, preferably Provençal

¼ cup slivered fresh basil

Provençal Vegetable Salad with Feta

Yield: 4–6 servings | Active time: 20 minutes | Start to finish: 1 hour

1. Combine salt and water in a large mixing bowl, and submerge eggplant slices; use a plate to press them down into the salted water. Soak eggplant for 30 minutes, then drain slices and squeeze to extract as much water as possible.

2. While eggplant soaks, prepare a medium-hot grill according to the instructions given in Chapter 1.

3. Place eggplant, zucchini, red bell pepper, onion, and mushrooms on a baking sheet, keeping vegetables segregated. Drizzle with oil and sprinkle with garlic, herbes de Provence, salt, and pepper. Turn vegetables to coat evenly.

4. Begin by placing onion and red bell pepper on the grill, and 4 minutes later add eggplant, zucchini, and mushrooms. Grill vegetables, covered, until tender and slightly brown, turning slices frequently. Vegetables should cook for a total of 10 minutes.

5. To serve, divide vegetables on individual plates or arrange on a platter. Sprinkle with vinegar, feta, olives, and basil. Serve hot or at room temperature.

Note: The vegetables can be grilled up to 4 hours in advance and kept at room temperature.

Chapter 6

Fish and Seafood

While shops selling only fish and seafood are disappearing from the scene, it is worth the effort to search your neighborhood for the best source you can find for fresh fish. Look for a market that offers a varied selection, that keeps its fish on foil placed on top of chipped ice, and that has a level of personal service that allows you to special-order specific varieties or cuts of fish. With the exception of Texas, there is not much water around the Southwestern states, but the assertive and bold flavors of the Southwest enhance many aquatic species imported to that area for grilling.

Spicy Southwest Shrimp

Yield: 4–6 servings | Active time: 25 minutes | Start to finish: 35 minutes

1. Prepare a medium-hot grill according to the instructions given in Chapter 1.

2. Using sharp scissors, cut along middle of the back of shrimp; leave tail and first segment intact. Devein shrimp using a sharp paring knife but do not remove shells. Rinse shrimp and pat dry with paper towels.

3. Place bacon in a large skillet over medium-high heat. Cook bacon until almost crisp, then add onion and garlic to the pan. Lower the heat to medium, and cook for 2 minutes, stirring constantly. Add chiles and cumin and continue to cook for 1 minute. Add tomato, beans, and stock. Bring to a boil, reduce the heat to low, and simmer mixture for 10 minutes. Add cilantro and thyme, and simmer 2 minutes. Season beans with salt, pepper, and lime juice, and keep hot.

4. Grill shrimp for 3–4 minutes per side, or until cooked through and opaque in the center. Serve shrimp on a bed of stewed beans.

Note: The bean mixture can be prepared 1 day in advance and refrigerated, tightly covered. Reheat it over low heat in a saucepan. Cook the shrimp just before serving.

Ingredients

- 2 pounds jumbo shrimp (less than 10 per pound), unpeeled
- ¼ pound bacon, finely sliced
- 2 medium onions, peeled and diced
- 5 garlic cloves, peeled and minced
- 3 jalapeño or serrano chiles, seeds and ribs removed, finely chopped
- 1 tablespoon ground cumin
- 2 medium tomatoes, cored, seeded, and diced
- 1 (15-ounce) can pinto beans, drained and rinsed
- 1 cup shrimp stock or bottled clam juice
- 2 tablespoons chopped fresh cilantro
- 2 teaspoons fresh thyme or ½ teaspoon dried
- Salt and freshly ground black pepper to taste
- Freshly squeezed lime juice to taste

2 pounds jumbo shrimp (less than 10 per pound), unpeeled

2 lemons

4 garlic cloves, peeled

Salt and freshly ground black pepper to taste

⅔ cup extra-virgin olive oil

¼ cup finely chopped fresh oregano

2 tablespoons chopped fresh parsley

Grilled Greek Shrimp

Yield: 4–6 servings | Active time: 20 minutes | Start to finish: 1 hour

1. Prepare a medium-hot grill according to the instructions given in Chapter 1.

2. Using sharp scissors, cut along middle of the back of shrimp; leave tail and first segment intact. Devein shrimp using a sharp paring knife but do not remove shells. Rinse shrimp and pat dry with paper towels.

3. Grate zest and squeeze juice from lemons. Combine lemon juice, lemon zest, garlic, salt, and pepper in a food processor fitted with a steel blade or in a blender. Puree until smooth, then add olive oil through the feed tube in a thin stream to create an emulsified dressing. Scrape dressing into a mixing bowl, and stir in oregano and parsley.

4. Pour half of dressing into a heavy resealable plastic bag, and add shrimp. Allow shrimp to marinate at room temperature for 10–15 minutes, turning the bag occasionally.

5. Grill shrimp, covered, for 3–4 minutes per side, or until cooked through and opaque in the center. Serve shrimp with remaining dressing.

VARIATIONS: *The same marinade works beautifully with large sea scallops or with fish fillets that are at least ⅔ inch thick. The cooking time will remain the same.*

Note: The dressing can be prepared up to 1 day in advance and refrigerated, tightly covered.

Grilled Greek Shrimp

Sea Scallops with Mango Salsa and Chile Vinaigrette

Yield: 6–8 servings | Active time: 25 minutes | Start to finish: 40 minutes

1. Soak bamboo skewers in warm water to cover, and prepare a medium-hot grill according to the instructions given in Chapter 1. Rinse scallops and pat dry with paper towels.

2. Combine mango, cucumber, onion, cilantro, 1 tablespoon olive oil, and lime juice in a glass or stainless-steel mixing bowl. Stir gently, and season to taste with salt and pepper. Allow salsa to sit at room temperature for at least 15 minutes to blend flavors.

3. Combine red pepper and vinegar in a food processor fitted with a steel blade or in a blender. With the motor running, slowly add remaining olive oil and chile oil through the feed tube to emulsify dressing. Season to taste with salt and pepper, and set aside.

4. Thread scallops onto two parallel skewers, sprinkle with salt and pepper, and brush with vinaigrette. Grill skewers, covered, for 1½–2 minutes per side. To serve, drizzle vinaigrette over skewers and place salsa next to them on the plate.

VARIATION: *Extra-large (16–20 per pound) shrimp or cubes of firm-fleshed white fish like cod or swordfish can be substituted for the scallops.*

Note: Both the salsa and the dressing can be made up to 1 day in advance and refrigerated, tightly covered. Allow both to reach room temperature before serving.

Ingredients:

- 12–16 (8-inch) bamboo skewers
- 2 pounds sea scallops
- 1 large, ripe mango, peeled, seeded, and cut into ¼-inch dice
- ½ small cucumber, peeled, seeded, and finely chopped
- ¼ small red onion, peeled and finely chopped
- 3 tablespoons chopped fresh cilantro
- ¾ cup olive oil, divided
- 2 tablespoons freshly squeezed lime juice
- Salt and freshly ground black pepper to taste
- 1 roasted red bell pepper, seeds and ribs removed, and diced
- ⅓ cup cider vinegar
- ¼–½ teaspoon Chinese chile oil, or to taste

Sea Scallops with Garden Relish

Yield: 4–6 servings | Active time: 20 minutes | Start to finish: 40 minutes

1. Soak bamboo skewers in warm water to cover, and prepare a medium-hot grill according to the instructions given in Chapter 1.

2. Rinse scallops and pat dry with paper towels. Brush scallops with 2 tablespoons oil, and sprinkle with salt and pepper.

3. Combine tomatoes, corn, scallions, and dill in a mixing bowl. Combine vinegar, sugar, salt, and pepper in a small bowl, and stir well. Add remaining oil, and stir well again. Toss dressing with vegetables, and set aside at room temperature.

4. Thread scallops onto two parallel skewers. Grill scallops for 3–4 minutes per side, uncovered if using a charcoal grill. To serve, place scallops on plates, and top with relish. Serve immediately.

Note: This dish can be served either hot or cold.

Ingredients:

- 8–12 (8-inch) bamboo skewers
- 24 large sea scallops
- ⅓ cup olive oil, divided
- Salt and freshly ground black pepper to taste
- 2 large ripe tomatoes, rinsed, cored, seeded, and chopped
- 1 cup fresh corn kernels, cooked
- 4 scallions, white parts and 2 inches of green tops, rinsed, trimmed, and thinly sliced
- 3 tablespoons chopped fresh dill
- ¼ cup white balsamic vinegar or cider vinegar
- 2 teaspoons granulated sugar

World's Easiest Fish

Yield: 4–6 servings | Active time: 15 minutes | Start to finish: 35 minutes

4–6 boneless (6–8-ounce) fish steaks or fillets of your choice, at least 1 inch thick

⅔ cup commercial mayonnaise

3 tablespoons chopped fresh herbs (such as oregano, rosemary, tarragon, basil, parsley, or some combination)

2 garlic cloves, peeled and minced

Salt and freshly ground black pepper to taste

1. Prepare a medium-hot grill according to the instructions given in Chapter 1.

2. Rinse fish and pat dry with paper towels. Combine mayonnaise, herbs, garlic, salt, and pepper in a mixing bowl, and stir well. Coat both sides of fish steaks with mixture.

3. Grill fish, uncovered if using a charcoal grill, for 3–5 minutes per side, or until cooked through and just slightly translucent in the center. Serve immediately.

Salmon with Spicy Pecan Butter

Yield: 4–6 servings | Active time: 25 minutes | Start to finish: 40 minutes

4–6 (6–8-ounce) salmon fillets

2 tablespoons olive oil

Salt and freshly ground black pepper to taste

1 jalapeño or serrano chile, seeds and ribs removed

¾ cup pecans, toasted in a 350°F oven for 5 minutes

4 sprigs fresh parsley

¼ pound (1 stick) unsalted butter, softened

2 tablespoons freshly squeezed lemon juice

1⅓ cups dry white wine

4 shallots, peeled and finely chopped

⅓ cup half-and-half

1. Prepare a medium-hot grill according to the instructions given in Chapter 1.

2. Rinse salmon, and pat dry with paper towels. Rub salmon with olive oil, sprinkle with salt and pepper, and set aside.

3. Combine chile, toasted pecans, parsley, butter, and lemon juice in a food processor fitted with a steel blade, and chop finely using on-and-off pulsing. Place wine and shallots in a small saucepan and reduce by half. Add half-and-half and reduce by half again. Slowly whisk in pecan mixture, and season to taste with salt and pepper.

4. Cook fish, covered, for 4–5 minutes per side, turning gently with a wide spatula, or until fish is opaque at the edges and slightly translucent in the center. Serve immediately, topped with butter sauce.

Note: The butter sauce can be made up to 4 hours in advance and kept hot in a warmed insulated bottle.

Aegean Swordfish

Yield: 4–6 servings | Active time: 15 minutes | Start to finish: 2¼ hours, including 2 hours for marinating

1. Rinse swordfish steaks and set aside. Combine wine, lemon zest, lemon juice, garlic, shallot, parsley, oregano, thyme, salt, and pepper in a heavy resealable plastic bag and mix well. Add olive oil, and mix well again. Add swordfish and marinate, refrigerated, for 2–3 hours, turning the bag occasionally.

2. Prepare a dual-temperature hot-and-medium grill according to the instructions given in Chapter 1.

3. Remove fish from marinade, and discard marinade. Sear fish for 2–3 minutes per side on the hot side of the grill, uncovered if using a charcoal grill, then transfer fish to the cooler side of the grill, and cook for an additional 2–3 minutes per side, or until slightly translucent in the center. Serve immediately.

Note: Other firm-fleshed fish such as sea bass, halibut, or scrod can be substituted.

4–6 (6–8-ounce) swordfish steaks

½ cup dry white wine

Grated zest from 1 lemon

¼ cup freshly squeezed lemon juice

4 garlic cloves, peeled and minced

1 shallot, peeled and chopped

¼ cup chopped fresh parsley

2 tablespoons dried oregano

1 tablespoon chopped fresh thyme or 1 teaspoon dried

Salt and freshly ground black pepper to taste

½ cup olive oil

Aegean Swordfish

4–6 (6–8-ounce) swordfish
 steaks

¼ cup olive oil

2 teaspoons dried oregano

Salt and freshly ground
 black pepper to taste

2 pounds ripe plum
 tomatoes

3 jalapeño or serrano
 chiles, stemmed

1 small onion, peeled and
 diced

3 garlic cloves, peeled and
 minced

¼ cup chopped fresh
 cilantro

Swordfish with Roasted Tomato Sauce

Yield: 4–6 servings | Active time: 25 minutes | Start to finish: 50 minutes

1. Prepare a dual-temperature hot-and-medium grill according to the instructions given in Chapter 1. Rinse swordfish, and pat dry with paper towels. Rub fish with oil, and sprinkle with oregano, salt, and pepper. Set aside.

2. Place tomatoes and chiles on the hot side of the grill, and cook until the skin is black, turning vegetables gently with tongs. Remove vegetables from the grill, and remove skin when cool enough to handle. Transfer tomatoes and chiles to a food processor fitted with a steel blade or to a blender. Add onion and garlic, and puree until smooth. Scrape sauce into a bowl, and stir in cilantro. Season to taste with salt and pepper, and set aside.

3. Sear fish for 2–3 minutes per side on the hot side of the grill, uncovered if using a charcoal grill, then transfer fish to the cooler side of the grill, and cook for an additional 2–3 minutes per side, or until slightly translucent in the center. Serve immediately, passing sauce separately.

Note: The sauce can be prepared up to 2 days in advance and refrigerated, tightly covered. Reheat it over low heat before using.

Chapter 7

Poultry

Famed nineteenth-century French gastronome, Jean Anthelme Brillat-Savarin, once wrote that "poultry is for the cook what canvas is for the painter." Its inherently mild flavor takes to myriad methods of seasoning, and it is relatively quick to cook too. Almost every permutation of chicken is now available in most supermarkets—from whole birds of various sizes to delicate breast tenderloins. However, there are times and reasons why knowing how to do some chicken cutting are advantageous, so here is a brief guide:

- **Pounding chicken breasts.** Some recipes will tell you to pound the breast to an even thickness so it will cook evenly and quickly. To do so, place the breast between two sheets of plastic wrap, and pound with the smooth side of a meat mallet or the bottom of a small, heavy skillet or saucepan.

- **Butterflying a whole chicken.** Butterflying is a process of partially boning a whole chicken so that it can be pressed down flat on the grill and will cook over direct heat, and therefore, in less time than if you kept it whole. Turn the chicken with the breast side down, and, using poultry shears, cut away the backbone from the tail to the head end on both sides, and discard the backbone (or save it for making stock). Open the bird by pulling the halves apart. Use a sharp paring knife to lightly score the top of the breastbone, then run your thumbs along and under the breastbone, and pull it out. Spread the bird flat. It's now time to turn the chicken over. Cut off the wing tips, and you are ready to grill.

4–6 (6-ounce) boneless skinless chicken breast halves

1 cup finely chopped fresh cilantro

⅓ cup freshly squeezed lime juice

2 garlic cloves, peeled and minced

1 tablespoon ground cumin

1 tablespoon chili powder

Salt and freshly ground black pepper to taste

⅔ cup olive oil

2 bell peppers of any color, seeds and ribs removed, and quartered

2 sweet onions, such as Vidalia or Bermuda, peeled and cut into ½-inch slices

8–12 (8-inch) flour tortillas

Salsa, guacamole, or sour cream (optional)

Chicken and Vegetable Fajitas

Yield: 4–6 servings | Active time: 25 minutes | Start to finish: 45 minutes, including 30 minutes for marinating

1. Prepare a hot grill according to the instructions given in Chapter 1.

2. Trim chicken breasts of all visible fat, and pound to an even thickness of ½ inch between two sheets of plastic wrap. Combine cilantro, lime juice, garlic, cumin, chili powder, salt, and pepper in a heavy resealable plastic bag; mix well. Add olive oil, and mix well again. Pour off half of mixture, and set aside. Add chicken breasts to remaining marinade, and turn to coat food evenly. Marinate chicken for 30 minutes at room temperature, turning bag occasionally.

3. While chicken is marinating, grill vegetables for a total of 10 to 12 minutes, or until tender, turning once. Remove vegetables from the grill, and when cool enough to handle, cut into thin strips.

4. Remove chicken from marinade, and discard marinade. Grill chicken for 2–3 minutes per side, uncovered, or until chicken is cooked through and no longer pink.

5. Grill tortillas for 1 minute per side, or until grill marks show. To serve, cut chicken crosswise into thin strips, and add to vegetable mixture. Drizzle mixture with some of remaining marinade. One tortilla at a time, place a portion of mixture on the bottom edge of tortilla. Fold over one side, and roll tortilla firmly but gently to enclose filling. Serve immediately, passing salsa, guacamole, or sour cream separately, if using.

VARIATION: *For beef fajitas, substitute flank steak or skirt steak for the chicken. Marinate the beef for 2 to 3 hours, refrigerated. Consult a similar recipe to determine the cooking time.*

Note: Marinade can be made up to 2 days in advance and refrigerated, tightly covered.

Chicken and Vegetable Fajitas

4 (10-ounce) chicken breast halves with skin and bones

Salt and freshly ground black pepper to taste

¼ pound Gruyère cheese, grated

¼ pound cooked ham, cut into ¼-inch dice

1 tablespoon fresh thyme or 1 teaspoon dried

3 tablespoons unsalted butter, melted

2 tablespoons freshly squeezed lemon juice

2 tablespoons Worcestershire sauce

Ham and Cheese–Stuffed Chicken

Yield: 4 servings | Active time: 15 minutes | Start to finish: 55 minutes

1. Prepare a medium-hot grill according to the instructions given in Chapter 1.

2. Rinse chicken and pat dry with paper towels. Insert a sharp paring knife into the thicker side of chicken breasts and cut a lengthwise pocket, being careful not to puncture the skin. Sprinkle chicken with salt and pepper, and set aside.

2. Combine cheese, ham, and thyme in a small bowl. Gently stuff mixture into pocket of chicken, and secure opening with a wooden toothpick or metal skewer. Combine butter, lemon juice, and Worcestershire sauce in a small bowl, and set aside.

3. Grill chicken, covered, for 10–12 minutes per side, basting it frequently with sauce. Do not baste for final 2 minutes of cooking, and discard any unused sauce. Chicken is cooked when it registers 160˚F on an instant-read thermometer inserted into the thickest part. Serve immediately.

VARIATION: *Cheddar cheese and cooked sausage can be substituted for the Gruyère and ham, and either stuffing can also be used for pork chops.*

---

4 (10-ounce) chicken breast halves with skin and bones

Salt and freshly ground black pepper to taste

2 garlic cloves, peeled

2 jalapeño or serrano chiles, stemmed

2 cups firmly packed fresh cilantro leaves

2 tablespoons olive oil

2 tablespoons freshly grated Parmesan cheese

6 ounces mild goat cheese, softened

Chicken Breasts Stuffed with Cilantro Goat Cheese

Yield: 4 servings | Active time: 15 minutes | Start to finish: 55 minutes

1. Prepare a medium-hot grill according to the instructions given in Chapter 1.

2. Rinse chicken and pat dry with paper towels. Insert a sharp paring knife into the thicker side of chicken breasts and cut a lengthwise pocket, being careful not to puncture the skin. Sprinkle chicken with salt and pepper, and set aside.

3. Combine garlic, chiles, cilantro, oil, Parmesan cheese, and goat cheese in a food processor fitted with a steel blade or in a blender. Puree until smooth, and season to taste with salt and pepper. Gently stuff mixture into pocket of chicken, and secure opening with a wooden toothpick or metal skewer.

4. Grill chicken, covered, for 10–12 minutes per side, turning gently with tongs. Chicken is cooked when it registers 160˚F on an instant-read thermometer inserted into the thickest part. Serve immediately.

Note: The cheese mixture can be prepared up to 2 days in advance and refrigerated, tightly covered.

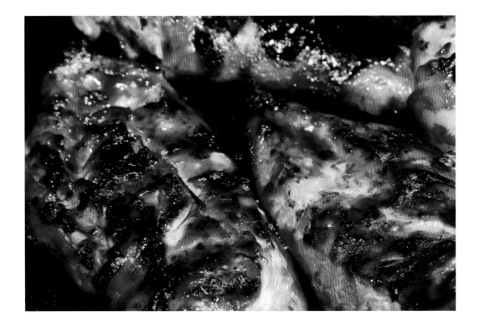

Mexican Chicken with
Mole Sauce

Mexican Chicken with Mole Sauce

Yield: 4–6 servings | Active time: 25 minutes | Start to finish: 50 minutes

1. Prepare a medium-hot grill according to the instructions given in Chapter 1.

2. Rinse chicken and pat dry with paper towels. Combine 3 tablespoons oil, 2 garlic cloves, and 2 tablespoons chili powder in a small bowl. Season to taste with salt and cayenne. Mix well, and rub mixture on chicken. Set aside.

3. Heat remaining 2 tablespoons oil in a heavy saucepan over medium-high heat. Add onions and remaining garlic and cook, stirring frequently, for 3 minutes or until onions are translucent. Stir in remaining chili powder and cumin and cook, stirring constantly, for 1 minute.

4. Add chicken stock, tomatoes, peanut butter, raisins, sugar, and cocoa powder. Stir well, and bring to a boil over high heat. Reduce the heat to low and simmer sauce for 15 minutes, or until slightly thickened. Season to taste with salt and cayenne.

5. Grill chicken, covered, starting with skin-side down for 8–10 minutes per side or until white meat registers 160°F and dark meat registers 165°F on an instant-read thermometer. Remove chicken from the grill, and serve immediately, passing sauce on the side.

VARIATION: *Pork chops can be substituted for the chicken pieces. Consult a similar recipe to determine the cooking time.*

Note: The sauce can be prepared up to 2 days in advance and refrigerated, tightly covered. Reheat over low heat, stirring occasionally.

4–8 chicken pieces of your choice (breasts, thighs, legs) with skin and bones

5 tablespoons olive oil

6 garlic cloves, peeled and minced

4 tablespoons chili powder

Salt and cayenne to taste

2 onions, peeled and chopped

2 teaspoons ground cumin

2 cups chicken stock

3 ripe plum tomatoes, rinsed, cored, seeded, and chopped

¼ cup peanut butter

¼ cup raisins

1 tablespoon granulated sugar

1 tablespoon unsweetened cocoa powder

2 (3-pound) whole chickens

¼ pound (1 stick) unsalted butter, softened

3 tablespoons chopped fresh parsley

2 tablespoons chopped fresh rosemary or 2 teaspoons dried

1 tablespoon chopped fresh thyme or 1 teaspoon dried

1 tablespoon grated lemon zest

Salt and freshly ground black pepper to taste

½ lemon, seeded and very thinly sliced

4 bricks, wrapped in heavy-duty aluminum foil

Butterflied Lemon-Herb Chicken

Yield: 4–6 servings | Active time: 20 minutes | Start to finish: 50 minutes

1. Rinse chickens and pat dry with paper towels. Butterfly chickens according to the instructions given above.

2. Prepare a medium-hot grill according to the instructions given in Chapter 1.

3. Combine butter, parsley, rosemary, thyme, lemon zest, salt, and pepper in a mixing bowl, and mix well. Stuff mixture under the skin of each chicken, being careful not to tear the skin. Lay lemon slices on top of herbed butter.

4. Place chickens over a medium fire skin-side down. Place 2 bricks on top of each chicken. Grill chicken, covered, for 10 minutes. Remove bricks, and turn chickens over. Replace bricks, and cook for an additional 12 minutes or until an instant-read thermometer registers 180°F when inserted into the thigh. Allow chickens to rest for 5 minutes, then cut into serving pieces, and serve immediately.

Note: Rather than using a whole chicken, you can make this dish with the individual parts of your choice. Consult a similar recipe to determine the cooking time.

Butterflied Lemon-Herb Chicken

Turkey Cutlets Ensalata

Yield: 6–8 servings | Active time: 15 minutes | Start to finish: 35 minutes

1. Prepare a hot grill according to the instructions given in Chapter 1.

2. Rinse turkey and pat dry with paper towels. Rub cutlets with 1 tablespoon olive oil, and sprinkle with Italian seasoning, salt, and pepper. Set aside. Combine vinegar, garlic, oregano, salt, and pepper in a jar with a tight-fitting lid, and shake well. Add remaining olive oil, and shake well again.

3. Grill turkey for 2–3 minutes per side, uncovered, or until turkey is cooked through and no longer pink. Remove turkey from the grill, and keep warm.

4. Combine tomatoes, radicchio, and scallions in a mixing bowl. Toss with dressing. To serve, top each cutlet with a portion of salad mixture, and serve immediately.

Note: The dressing can be prepared up to 1 day in advance and refrigerated, tightly covered. Allow it to reach room temperature before using.

6–8 turkey breast cutlets, about ½ inch thick

¼ cup olive oil, divided

2 teaspoons Italian seasoning

Salt and freshly ground black pepper to taste

¼ cup balsamic vinegar

2 garlic cloves, peeled and minced

1 tablespoon chopped fresh oregano or 1 teaspoon dried

1½ cups chopped fresh plum tomatoes

1 cup finely chopped radicchio

2 scallions, white parts only, trimmed and chopped

Duck with Spiced Citrus Chile Sauce

Yield: 4 servings | Active time: 25 minutes | Start to finish: 1 hour

1. Prepare a medium-hot grill according to the instructions given in Chapter 1.

2. Rinse duck breasts and pat dry with paper towels. Trim off all extra skin, and score the remaining skin in a diamond pattern, being careful not to cut into the flesh beneath the skin. Sprinkle duck with salt and pepper, and set aside.

3. Combine orange juice, lime juice, honey, chile, cinnamon stick, and cloves in a small saucepan and bring to a boil over medium-high heat, stirring occasionally. Reduce the heat to medium and cook sauce until it is reduced by half. Strain sauce and discard solids. Season sauce to taste with salt and pepper, and keep warm.

4. Grill duck breasts skin-side down, uncovered if using a charcoal grill, for 7 minutes, or until skin is browned. Turn duck gently with tongs, and grill other side for 3–4 minutes. Remove duck from grill, and allow it to rest for 5 minutes, lightly covered with aluminum foil. Slice each breast into ½-inch slices on the diagonal, and serve immediately, passing sauce separately.

Note: The sauce can be cooked up to 1 day in advance and refrigerated, tightly covered. Reheat over low heat, stirring occasionally.

4 (7-ounce) boneless duck breast halves with skin

Salt and freshly ground black pepper

2½ cups freshly squeezed orange juice

¼ cup freshly squeezed lime juice

3 tablespoons honey

1 jalapeño or serrano chile, stemmed and halved

1 cinnamon stick

2 whole cloves

Chapter 8

Beef and Venison

Of course there is a chapter in this book about cooking beef—after all, steaks on the grill are part and parcel of life if you list yourself amongst the ranks of carnivores. Even on a gas grill, the aroma and flavor of a grilled steak is unsurpassed. And in the Southwest, beef is king. It is only in the past few decades that farm-raised game has been available to home cooks and not just restaurant chefs. That has placed such culinary wonders as lean, healthful venison in supermarkets, and you will find some recipes for that meat in this chapter, too.

4–6 (10-ounce) New York strip or boneless rib eye steaks

1 tablespoon herbes de Provence

1 tablespoon dry mustard

4 garlic cloves, peeled and minced

Salt and freshly ground black pepper to taste

4 ears fresh corn, shucked

2 tablespoons olive oil

1 small onion, peeled and diced

1 red bell pepper, seeds and ribs removed, and finely chopped

3 tablespoons chili powder

½ cup dry red wine

3 cups beef stock

½ cup heavy cream

Grilled Steak with Southwestern Corn Sauce
Yield: 4–6 servings | Active time: 25 minutes | Start to finish: 45 minutes

1. Prepare a dual-temperature hot-and-medium grill according to the instructions given in Chapter 1. Rinse steaks and pat dry with paper towels. Combine herbes de Provence, mustard, garlic, salt, and pepper in a small bowl. Rub mixture on both sides of steaks.

2. Cut kernels from corn using a sharp serrated knife. Place one-quarter of kernels in a food processor fitted with a steel blade or in a blender and puree until smooth. Heat oil in a saucepan over medium-high heat. Add onion and red pepper and cook, stirring frequently, for 3 minutes, or until onion is translucent. Add chili powder and stir over low heat for 1 minute. Add wine, stock, and pureed corn to the pan, and boil over medium heat, stirring occasionally, until the mixture is reduced by half. Add cream and corn kernels to sauce and cook over medium heat for 5 minutes, stirring occasionally. Season to taste with salt and pepper, and keep hot.

3. Sear steaks over the hot side of the grill for 2–3 minutes per side, uncovered if using a charcoal grill. Transfer steaks to the cooler side of the grill and cook for an additional 5–7 minutes, uncovered if using a charcoal grill, or to desired doneness. Allow steaks to rest for 5 minutes. To serve, slice steaks into ¾-inch slices and top with sauce. Serve immediately.

VARIATION: *The same sauce made with chicken stock rather than beef stock and white wine rather than red wine works very well on chicken or pork chops. Consult a similar recipe to determine cooking time.*

Note: The sauce can be prepared up to 1 day in advance and refrigerated, tightly covered. Allow it to reach room temperature before using.

Steak with Marsala Mushroom Sauce

Yield: 4–6 servings | Active time: 20 minutes | Start to finish: 45 minutes

1. Prepare a dual-temperature hot-and-medium grill according to the instructions given in Chapter 1. Rinse steaks and pat dry with paper towels. Sprinkle steaks with salt and pepper.

2. Heat oil and butter in a large skillet over medium-high heat. Add shallots and garlic and cook, stirring frequently, for 3 minutes, or until shallots are translucent. Add mushrooms and cook, stirring frequently, for 5 minutes. Add Marsala, stock, parsley, and thyme. Bring to a boil, and cook, stirring occasionally, until sauce is reduced by two-thirds. Season to taste with salt and pepper, and keep warm.

3. Sear steaks over the hot side of the grill for 2–3 minutes per side, uncovered if using a charcoal grill. Transfer steaks to the cooler side of the grill and cook for an additional 5–7 minutes, uncovered if using a charcoal grill, or to desired doneness. Allow steaks to rest for 5 minutes. To serve, slice steaks into ¾-inch slices and top with sauce. Serve immediately.

VARIATION: *Veal loin chops are also delicious with this sauce, as are chicken breasts.*

Note: The sauce can be prepared up to 1 day in advance and refrigerated, tightly covered. Reheat it over low heat before using.

4–6 (10-ounce) New York strip or boneless rib eye steaks

Salt and freshly ground black pepper to taste

¼ cup olive oil

3 tablespoons unsalted butter

3 shallots, peeled and minced

3 garlic cloves, peeled and minced

¾ pound mushrooms, wiped with a damp paper towel and sliced

1½ cups Marsala wine

½ cup beef stock

¼ cup chopped fresh parsley

1 tablespoon chopped fresh thyme or 1 teaspoon dried

Steak with Marsala Mushroom Sauce

4–6 (10-ounce) New York strip or boneless rib eye steaks

1 cup dry red wine

¼ cup red wine vinegar

1 small onion, peeled and chopped

4 garlic cloves, peeled and minced, divided

1 large jalapeño or serrano chile, seeds and ribs removed, and finely chopped

2 tablespoons ground cumin

1 tablespoon dried oregano, preferably Mexican, divided

Salt to taste

½ cup olive oil

½ cup mayonnaise

1 chipotle chile in adobo sauce, finely chopped

2 teaspoons adobo sauce

Steaks with Chipotle Mayonnaise

Yield: 4–6 servings | Active time: 20 minutes | Start to finish: 3½ hours, including 3 hours for marinating

1. Rinse steaks and pat dry with paper towels. Combine wine, vinegar, onion, 3 garlic cloves, chile, cumin, and 2½ teaspoons oregano in a heavy resealable plastic bag. Add salt to taste, and mix well. Add olive oil, and mix well again. Add steaks and marinate, refrigerated, for 3–5 hours, turning the bag occasionally.

2. Prepare a dual-temperature hot-and-medium grill according to the instructions given in Chapter 1. Combine mayonnaise, chipotle chile, adobo sauce, remaining garlic, and remaining oregano in a mixing bowl. Whisk well.

3. Sear steaks over the hot side of the grill for 2–3 minutes per side, uncovered if using a charcoal grill. Transfer steaks to the cooler side of the grill and cook for an additional 5–7 minutes, uncovered if using a charcoal grill, or to desired doneness. Allow steaks to rest for 5 minutes. To serve, slice steaks into ¾-inch slices and top with sauce. Serve immediately.

VARIATION: *Lamb loin chops are also delicious with this sauce, as are chicken breasts.*

Note: The sauce can be prepared up to 1 day in advance and refrigerated, tightly covered.

4–6 (10-ounce) New York strip or boneless rib eye steaks

Salt and freshly ground black pepper to taste

¼ cup Worcestershire sauce

1 tablespoon red wine vinegar

1 tablespoon Dijon mustard

2 large shallots, peeled and minced

2 garlic cloves, peeled and minced

3 tablespoons chopped fresh parsley

2 tablespoons chopped fresh oregano or 2 teaspoons dried

1 tablespoon chopped fresh rosemary or 1 teaspoon dried

1 tablespoon chopped fresh thyme or 1 teaspoon dried

⅓ cup extra-virgin olive oil

Steak with Herb Sauce

Yield: 4–6 servings | Active time: 25 minutes | Start to finish: 40 minutes

1. Prepare a dual-temperature hot-and-medium grill according to the instructions given in Chapter 1. Rinse steaks and pat dry with paper towels. Sprinkle steaks with salt and pepper.

2. Combine Worcestershire sauce, vinegar, mustard, shallots, garlic, parsley, oregano, rosemary, thyme, salt, and pepper in a jar with a tight-fitting lid, and shake well. Add olive oil, and shake well again. Set aside.

3. Sear steaks over the hot side of the grill for 2–3 minutes per side, uncovered if using a charcoal grill. Transfer steaks to the cooler side of the grill and cook for an additional 5–7 minutes, uncovered if using a charcoal grill, or to desired doneness. Allow steaks to rest for 5 minutes. To serve, slice steaks into ¾-inch slices and top with sauce. Serve immediately.

Note: The sauce can be prepared up to 1 day in advance and refrigerated, tightly covered. Allow it to reach room temperature before using.

Steak with Tuscan Parmesan Butter

Yield: 4–6 servings | Active time: 20 minutes | Start to finish: 45 minutes

1. Prepare a dual-temperature hot-and-medium grill according to the instructions given in Chapter 1. Rinse steaks and pat dry with paper towels.

2. Combine olive oil, garlic, rosemary, salt, and pepper in a small bowl, and mix well. Rub mixture on both sides of steaks, and set aside.

3. Combine butter, Parmesan, paprika, mustard, salt, and pepper in another small bowl, and mix well. Form mixture into a log with a sheet of plastic wrap, and chill until ready to use.

4. Sear steaks over the hot side of the grill for 2–3 minutes per side, uncovered if using a charcoal grill. Transfer steaks to the cooler side of the grill and cook for an additional 6–8 minutes, uncovered if using a charcoal grill, for rare, or to desired doneness. Allow steaks to rest for 5 minutes. To serve, slice steaks into ¾-inch slices and top each serving with a pat of seasoned butter. Serve immediately.

Note: The butter topping can be prepared up to 1 day in advance and refrigerated, tightly covered.

2 (2-pound) T-bone or porterhouse steaks, about 2 inches thick

¼ cup olive oil

5 garlic cloves, peeled and minced

2 tablespoons chopped fresh rosemary or 2 teaspoons dried

Salt and freshly ground black pepper to taste

4 tablespoons (½ stick) unsalted butter, softened

¼ cup freshly grated Parmesan cheese

1 tablespoon Spanish smoked paprika

2 teaspoons Dijon mustard

Steak with Tuscan Parmesan Butter

1 (2-pound) flank steak

¼ cup soy sauce

¼ cup dry red wine

1 tablespoon Dijon
mustard

2 tablespoons chopped
fresh basil, preferably
Thai basil, or 2 teaspoons
dried

6 garlic cloves, peeled and
minced

2 tablespoons chopped
fresh cilantro

½ teaspoon crushed red
pepper flakes or to taste

Salt to taste

¼ cup olive oil

Garlicky Flank Steak

Yield: 4–6 servings | Active time: 15 minutes | Start to finish: 3½ hours, including 3 hours for marinating

1. Rinse flank steak and pat dry with paper towels. Score steak lightly on both sides with a paring knife in a diamond pattern ¼-inch deep. Combine soy sauce, wine, mustard, basil, garlic, cilantro, red pepper flakes, and salt in a heavy resealable plastic bag. Mix well, add olive oil, and mix well again. Add steak to marinade and marinate, refrigerated, for a minimum of 3 hours and up to 8 hours, turning the bag occasionally.

2. Prepare a hot grill according to the instructions given in Chapter 1.

3. Grill steak, uncovered if using a charcoal grill, for 3–4 minutes per side for medium-rare or to desired doneness. Allow steak to rest for 5 minutes, then carve into slices. Serve immediately.

Note: The marinade can be prepared up to 1 day in advance and refrigerated, tightly covered.

Garlicky Flank Steak

Steak, Potato, and Mushroom Kebabs

Yield: 4–6 servings | Active time: 25 minutes | Start to finish: 3 hours, including 2 hours for marinating

1. Soak bamboo skewers in warm water to cover. Rinse beef and pat dry with paper towels. Cut beef into 1½-inch cubes. Remove and discard mushroom stems. Wipe mushrooms clean with a damp paper towel. Cut each mushroom into 8 chunks.

2. Combine wine, vinegar, garlic, rosemary, thyme, salt, and pepper in a heavy resealable plastic bag, and mix well. Add olive oil, and mix well again. Add beef and mushrooms to the bag, and marinate, refrigerated, for 2 hours or up to 4 hours, turning the bag occasionally.

3. Place potatoes in a saucepan of salted water. Bring to a boil over high heat, and boil potatoes for 10 minutes, or until barely tender. Drain potatoes, and plunge into ice water to stop the cooking action. When cool enough to handle, cut potatoes in half, or quarter them if larger than 3 inches in diameter. Set aside.

4. Prepare a dual-temperature hot-and-medium grill according to the instructions given in Chapter 1.

5. Remove meat and mushrooms from marinade, and discard marinade. Thread beef, mushroom sections, and potatoes onto two parallel skewers.

6. Sear kebabs on the hot side of the grill for 1½ minutes, turning them in quarter turns, uncovered if using a charcoal grill, on the hot side of the grill. Then transfer skewers to cooler side of the grill, and cook for a total of 6 minutes more for medium-rare, or to desired doneness. Serve immediately.

VARIATION: *Cubes of boneless leg of lamb are also delicious with this recipe.*

Note: The marinade can be prepared and the potatoes can be boiled 1 day in advance and refrigerated, tightly covered.

8–12 (8-inch) bamboo skewers

2 pounds sirloin tips

2 large portobello mushrooms

¾ cup dry red wine

¼ cup balsamic vinegar

2 garlic cloves, peeled and minced

3 tablespoons chopped fresh rosemary or 1 tablespoon dried

1 tablespoon chopped fresh thyme or 1 teaspoon dried

Salt and freshly ground black pepper to taste

⅓ cup olive oil

1 pound small new potatoes, scrubbed

1 (2-pound) flank steak

4 garlic cloves, peeled

1 jalapeño or serrano chile, stemmed

½ cup firmly packed fresh cilantro leaves

1/3 cup freshly squeezed orange juice

¼ cup freshly squeezed lime juice

Salt and freshly ground black pepper to taste

½ cup olive oil

12–16 (6-inch) corn tortillas

Shredded iceberg lettuce, chopped onion, grated Monterey Jack cheese, and Pico de Gallo (recipe on page 104)

Southwestern Steak Tacos

Yield: 6–8 servings | Active time: 20 minutes | Start to finish: 3½ hours, including 3 hours for marinating

1. Rinse flank steak and pat dry with paper towels. Score steak lightly on both sides in a diamond pattern ¼-inch deep. Combine garlic, chile, cilantro, orange juice, lime juice, salt, and pepper in a blender or food processor fitted with a steel blade. Puree until smooth. Add olive oil, and mix well. Pour marinade into a heavy resealable plastic bag, add steak, and marinate, refrigerated, for a minimum of 3 hours and up to 8 hours, turning the bag occasionally.

2. Prepare a hot grill according to the instructions given in Chapter 1.

3. Grill steak, uncovered if using a charcoal grill, for 3–4 minutes per side for medium-rare or to desired doneness. Allow steak to rest for 5 minutes, then carve into slices. While steak rests, warm tortillas on the grill. Divide beef on top of tortillas, and serve immediately, passing bowls of lettuce, onion, cheese, and Pico de Gallo separately.

Note: The marinade can be prepared up to 1 day in advance and refrigerated, tightly covered.

4–6 (6-ounce) boneless venison steaks, cut from the loin

2 cups dry red wine, divided

2 shallots, peeled and chopped

4 garlic cloves, peeled and minced, divided

2 tablespoons chopped fresh cilantro

2 tablespoons chopped fresh oregano or 2 teaspoons dried

Salt and freshly ground black pepper to taste

½ cup olive oil

2 tablespoons vegetable oil

1 small red onion, peeled and chopped

2 jalapeño or serrano chiles, seeds and ribs removed, and chopped

4 cups beef stock

½ cup frozen orange juice concentrate, thawed

¼ cup firmly packed dark brown sugar

1 tablespoon grated orange zest

Venison with Citrus Jalapeño Sauce

Yield: 4–6 servings | Active time: 25 minutes | Start to finish: 8½ hours, including 8 hours for marinating

1. Rinse venison and pat dry with paper towels. Place venison between two sheets of plastic wrap and pound to an even thickness of 1/3 inch. Combine 1 cup wine, shallots, 2 garlic cloves, cilantro, oregano, salt, and pepper in a heavy resealable plastic bag, and mix well. Add olive oil, and mix well again. Add venison, and marinate, refrigerated, for at least 8 hours or up to 24 hours, turning the bag occasionally.

2. While venison marinates, make sauce. Heat vegetable oil in a large saucepan over medium-high heat. Add remaining garlic, onions, and chiles and cook, stirring frequently, for 3 minutes or until onion is translucent. Add remaining wine and cook until only ¼ cup remains. Add beef stock and cook until reduced by three-quarters. Whisk in orange juice concentrate, sugar, and orange zest, and cook for 10 minutes, stirring frequently. Season to taste with salt and pepper, and keep warm.

3. Prepare a hot grill according to the instructions given in Chapter 1.

4. Remove venison from marinade, and discard marinade. Sear venison for 2–3 minutes per side, uncovered if using a charcoal grill. Top steaks with sauce, and serve immediately.

Note: The sauce can be prepared up to 1 day in advance and refrigerated, tightly covered. Reheat it over low heat before using.

Venison Steaks with Red Wine Sauce

Yield: 4–6 servings | Active time: 20 minutes | Start to finish: 8½ hours, including 8 hours for marinating

1. Rinse venison and pat dry with paper towels. Place venison between two sheets of plastic wrap and pound to an even thickness of ⅓ inch. Combine 1½ cups wine, shallots, garlic, parsley, thyme, bay leaves, salt, and pepper in a heavy resealable plastic bag, and mix well. Add olive oil, and mix well again. Add venison, and marinate, refrigerated, for at least 8 hours or up to 24 hours, turning the bag occasionally.

2. Prepare a hot grill according to the instructions given in Chapter 1.

3. Heat 2 tablespoons butter and vegetable oil in a saucepan over medium-high heat. Add scallions and cook, stirring frequently, for 2 minutes, or until scallions are translucent. Raise the heat to high, and add remaining 1½ cups wine and brandy. Reduce over high heat, stirring occasionally, until only ⅔ cup remains. Cut remaining butter into small pieces, and whisk butter into sauce. Season to taste with salt and pepper, and set aside.

4. Remove venison from marinade and discard marinade. Sear venison for 2–3 minutes per side, uncovered if using a charcoal grill. Top steaks with sauce, and serve immediately.

Note: The sauce can be prepared up to 1 day in advance and refrigerated, tightly covered. Reheat it over low heat before using.

Ingredients

- 4–6 (6-ounce) boneless venison steaks, cut from the loin
- 3 cups dry red wine, divided
- 2 shallots, peeled and chopped
- 2 garlic cloves, peeled and minced
- 2 tablespoons chopped fresh parsley
- 1 tablespoon chopped fresh thyme or 1 teaspoon dried
- 2 bay leaves
- Salt and freshly ground black pepper to taste
- ½ cup olive oil
- 4 tablespoons (½ stick) unsalted butter, divided
- 2 tablespoons vegetable oil
- 6 scallions, white parts only, trimmed and chopped
- 2 tablespoons brandy

Chapter 9

Lamb, Pork, and Veal

During the mid-twentieth century, when I was first exposed to fine dining, the white-tablecloth restaurants in this country were termed "continental," and one of the dishes of note was always shish kebab; sometimes it even arrived on swords rather than skewers. It was one of the few ways that many Americans enjoyed eating lamb. The same menu would frequently include some Italian veal dishes, although most likely covered in cheese, and little pork other than the occasional ham steak topped with a ring of canned pineapple.

But all of that has changed, and while beef will probably always remain the king of red meats, lamb is now growing in popularity due to its rich, rosy flavor. And both pork and veal, now dubbed "the other white meats," are flavorful and tender alternatives to chicken.

Years ago there were butcher shops as well as butchers in every store to fulfill any special needs you might have for a cut of meat. However, that is no longer the case, so there are a few tasks formerly performed by butchers that it is good to know how to do. Here are the two main ones:

- **Trimming a pork tenderloin.** Pork tenderloins usually come in packages of two, each weighing between ¾ pound and 1 pound. The first task is to use the blade of a paring knife to scrape away the fat and very thin membrane coating the entire tenderloin. After this is accomplished you will see a stripe of iridescent white running from about halfway up the tenderloin to the thick end; this is the silver skin, and it should be removed so that the tenderloin will cook without curling. It is also very tough and gristly if eaten. Hold the end of the silver skin at the thin end with one hand, and insert a paring knife under it. Scrape it away from the meat, and repeat the process until all the silver skin has been removed.

- **Butterflying a leg of lamb.** It is now rather easy to find a boneless leg of lamb, but to grill successfully it has to lie much flatter on the grill. Remove the netting encasing it, or cut the strings creating its cylindrical shape. Roll out the meat, and you will have parts of various thicknesses ranging from almost no meat to an area about 6 inches thick. Start by cutting away large areas of fat, and trim the solid fat coating, called the fell, on what would have been the top of the leg to an even thickness of ¼ inch. Holding your knife parallel to the counter, start slicing the thicker areas of the lamb, pulling them open as if you were rolling out a sheet of piecrust. When all the meat is basically flat, cover the lamb with a sheet of plastic wrap, and pound it to an even thickness of 2 inches with the bottom of a small skillet or the flat side of a meat mallet.

Southwestern Pork Ribs

Yield: 4–6 servings | Active time: 20 minutes | Start to finish: 4 hours

1. If using a charcoal grill, soak mesquite chips in water for 30 minutes. If using a gas grill, create a packet for wood chips as described in Chapter 1. Rinse ribs, and pat dry with paper towels. Cut each slab in half. Rub both sides of ribs with spice rub, and allow to sit at room temperature.

2. Prepare a grill for indirect cooking as described in Chapter 1, pushing the coals to one side rather than around the periphery if using a charcoal grill, and lighting the burners on only one side if using a gas grill.

3. Drain wood chips, and sprinkle on coals, or place packet of wood chips under grate on burners. Place ribs on the cool side of the grill, and cook for 2 hours, covered, turning the slabs every 30 minutes to cook evenly. Add more charcoal to fire after 1 hour.

4. Move ribs to hot part of grill, and baste with barbecue sauce. Cook for 5–7 minutes per side, or until ribs are browned. Remove ribs from the grill, wrap slabs in heavy-duty aluminum foil, and let them rest for 45 minutes.

5. Reheat foil packets on the cool side of the grill, if necessary, then cut ribs into servings, and serve immediately. Pass extra sauce separately.

2 cups mesquite chips

2 slabs pork spareribs (about 6½ pounds)

¼ cup Tex-Mex Rub (recipe on page 7) or any spice rub of your choice

2 cups Southwestern Barbecue Sauce (recipe on page 21) or any barbecue sauce of your choice

Southwestern Pork Ribs

2 (¾-pound) pork tenderloins, trimmed of fat and silver skin as described above

⅓ cup olive oil, divided

4 garlic cloves, peeled and minced, divided

1 tablespoon paprika

1 tablespoon dried sage

Salt and freshly ground black pepper to taste

1 onion, peeled and chopped

½ cup freshly squeezed orange juice

½ cup ketchup

½ cup peach preserves

¼ cup cider vinegar

1 tablespoon Worcestershire sauce

½ teaspoon hot red pepper sauce, or to taste

Peach-Glazed Pork Tenderloin

Yield: 4–6 servings | Active time: 25 minutes | Start to finish: 50 minutes

1. Place pork in a baking dish. Combine 2 tablespoons olive oil, 2 garlic cloves, paprika, sage, salt, and pepper in a small bowl, and stir well. Rub paste on pork, and allow pork to sit at room temperature while the grill heats.

2. Prepare a dual-temperature hot-and-medium grill according to the instructions given in Chapter 1.

3. Heat remaining oil in a saucepan over medium-high heat. Add onion and remaining garlic and cook, stirring frequently, for 3 minutes, or until onions are translucent. Add orange juice, ketchup, peach preserves, vinegar, and Worcestershire sauce to the pan, and whisk well. Bring to a boil, and then reduce the heat to low. Simmer sauce, uncovered, for 15 minutes, stirring occasionally. Season to taste with salt and hot red pepper sauce. Transfer one-third of sauce to a small bowl for basting pork, and keep remaining sauce warm.

4. Grill pork, uncovered if using a charcoal grill, on the hot side of the grill for 2–3 minutes per side, turning it in quarter turns, and then move pork to the cooler side of the grill. Grill for an additional 5–6 minutes per side, basting with sauce, for medium. Allow pork to rest for 5 minutes, then slice pork on the diagonal into ½-inch slices, and pass extra sauce separately.

Note: The sauce can be prepared up to 2 days in advance and refrigerated, tightly covered. Reheat it over low heat before using.

6–8 (1-inch-thick) bone-in pork chops

Salt and freshly ground black pepper to taste

5 garlic cloves, peeled and minced, divided

3 tablespoons dried sage

Pinch of ground allspice

2 ripe mangoes, peeled and coarsely chopped

⅓ cup freshly squeezed lime juice

1 jalapeño or serrano chile, seeds and ribs removed, and diced

1 tablespoon grated orange zest

2 tablespoons olive oil

3 tablespoons chopped fresh cilantro

Cuban Pork Chops with Mango Sauce

Yield: 6–8 servings | Active time: 15 minutes | Start to finish: 35 minutes

1. Prepare a dual-temperature hot-and-medium grill according to the instructions given in Chapter 1.

2. Rinse pork chops and pat dry with paper towels. Sprinkle pork chops with salt and pepper. Combine 2 garlic cloves, sage, and allspice in a small bowl, and rub mixture on both sides of chops.

3. Combine mangoes, lime juice, remaining garlic, chile, orange zest, and olive oil in a food processor fitted with a steel blade or in a blender. Puree until smooth. Stir in cilantro, and season to taste with salt and pepper. Set aside.

4. Grill chops, uncovered if using a charcoal grill, on the hot side of the grill for 2–3 minutes per side and then move them to the cooler side of the grill. Grill for an additional 5–6 minutes per side for medium. Allow chops to rest for 5 minutes, then serve immediately, passing sauce separately.

Note: The sauce can be made up to 2 days in advance and refrigerated, tightly covered. Bring it to room temperature before using.

Lemon-Herb Veal Chops

Yield: 6 servings | Active time: 15 minutes | Start to finish: 4½ hours, including 4 hours for marinating

1. Rinse veal chops and pat dry with paper towels. Combine lemon juice with ¼ cup parsley, 2 tablespoons rosemary, thyme, 2 garlic cloves, shallot, salt, and pepper in a heavy resealable plastic bag, and mix well. Add olive oil, and mix well again. Add chops and marinate, refrigerated, for 4–6 hours, turning the bag occasionally.

2. While chops are marinating, combine remaining parsley, remaining rosemary, remaining garlic, and lemon zest in a small bowl. Mix well, and set aside.

3. Prepare a dual-temperature hot-and-medium grill according to the instructions given in Chapter 1.

4. Remove chops from marinade, discard marinade, and pat chops dry with paper towels. Grill chops on the hot side of the grill, uncovered if using a charcoal grill, for 3–4 minutes per side, then move them to the cooler side of the grill and cook for 4–5 minutes per side for medium or to desired doneness. Transfer chops to a platter or individual plates, and allow chops to rest for 5 minutes. Then sprinkle each with a few teaspoons of topping, and serve immediately.

VARIATION: *Thick pork chops are also delicious when soaked in this marinade.*

6 (1-inch-thick) veal chops

⅓ cup freshly squeezed lemon juice

½ cup chopped fresh parsley, divided

¼ cup chopped fresh rosemary, divided

1 tablespoon chopped fresh thyme or 1 teaspoon dried

3 garlic cloves, peeled and minced, divided

1 shallot, peeled and chopped

Salt and freshly ground black pepper to taste

½ cup olive oil

1 tablespoon grated lemon zest

Lemon-Herb Veal Chops

Moroccan Lamb Chops

Middle Eastern Lamb Kebabs with Greek Feta Sauce

Yield: 6–8 servings | Active time: 20 minutes | Start to finish: 1½ hours, including 1 hour for marinating

1. Rinse lamb, and pat dry with paper towels. Combine wine, shallots, garlic, oregano, cinnamon, salt, and pepper in a heavy resealable plastic bag, and mix well. Add olive oil, and mix well again. Add lamb, and marinate for 1 hour at room temperature or up to 6 hours refrigerated, turning the bag occasionally.

2. Soak bamboo skewers in warm water to cover, and prepare a medium-hot grill according to the instructions given in Chapter 1.

3. Remove lamb from marinade, and discard marinade. Thread lamb onto 2 parallel skewers. Grill lamb, uncovered, for 2–3 minutes per side, turning it in quarter turns, for medium-rare. Serve immediately, passing Greek Feta Sauce separately.

3 pounds boneless leg of lamb, fat trimmed, cut into 1-inch cubes

1 cup dry red wine

2 shallots, peeled and chopped

4 garlic cloves, peeled and minced

2 tablespoons dried oregano

½ teaspoon ground cinnamon

Salt and freshly ground black pepper to taste

½ cup olive oil

12–16 (8-inch) bamboo skewers

Greek Feta Sauce (recipe on page 22)

Moroccan Lamb Chops

Yield: 4–6 servings | Active time: 15 minutes | Start to finish: 1¼ hours, including 1 hour for marinating

1. Rinse lamb and pat dry with paper towels. Combine olive oil, cilantro, garlic, paprika, coriander, cumin, salt, and pepper in a heavy resealable plastic bag, and mix well. Add chops, coating them well with mixture. Marinate chops at room temperature for 1 hour, turning the bag occasionally, or up to 6 hours refrigerated.

2. Prepare a medium-hot grill according to the instructions given in Chapter 1.

3. Remove lamb chops from marinade, and discard marinade.

4. Grill chops, covered, for 3 minutes per side for medium-rare or to desired doneness. Serve immediately.

Note: The lamb chops can be grilled up to 1 day in advance and refrigerated, tightly covered. Reheat them in a single layer in a 450°F oven for 3 minutes per side, or until heated through.

2 (8-rib) racks of lamb, cut into 1-rib serving pieces

½ cup olive oil

1 cup chopped fresh cilantro

4 garlic cloves, peeled and minced

1 tablespoon paprika

1 tablespoon ground coriander

1 teaspoon ground cumin

Salt and freshly ground black pepper to taste

Chapter 10

Burgers of All Types

The beef hamburger is iconic of American cuisine—both in this country and around the world. There is no clear parentage, however, to the all-American hamburger placed between two slices of some sort of bread. One source vying for the title is Athens, Texas, also known for its black-eyed pea festival. Athens native Fletcher Davis, "Old Dave" to his friends, opened a lunch counter in the town in the 1880s, and introduced it to the nation at the St. Louis World's Fair in 1904.

1¾ pounds ground turkey

6 scallions, white parts and 3 inches green tops, rinsed, trimmed, and chopped

4 garlic cloves, peeled and minced

3 tablespoons chopped fresh cilantro

2 teaspoons finely chopped chipotle chiles in adobo sauce

1 teaspoon adobo sauce

2 teaspoons ground cumin

Salt and freshly ground black pepper to taste

4–6 rolls of your choice, sliced in half

½ cup Guacamole (recipe on page 103) or purchased guacamole

½ cup Summer Tomato Salsa (recipe on page 102) or purchased refrigerated salsa (do not use bottled salsa)

Lettuce and thinly sliced red onion

Spicy Southwestern Turkey Burgers

Yield: 4–6 servings | Active time: 15 minutes | Start to finish: 45 minutes

1. Prepare a dual-temperature hot-and-medium grill according to the instructions given in Chapter 1.

2. Combine turkey, scallions, garlic, cilantro, chipotle chiles, adobo sauce, cumin, salt, and pepper in a mixing bowl, and mix gently. Form mixture into 4–6 (¾-inch-thick) burgers.

3. Grill rolls on the hot side of the grill cut-side down until toasted. Sear burgers over high heat for 2 minutes per side, uncovered if using a charcoal grill, and then transfer burgers to the cooler side of the grill. Continue to cook, covered, for 3–5 minutes per side or until burgers register 160°F on an instant-read thermometer and are cooked through and no longer pink.

4. Serve immediately topped with guacamole, salsa, lettuce, and onion.

VARIATION: *Ground pork or ground veal can be substituted for the turkey. Cook these meats to desired doneness.*

Note: The turkey mixture can be prepared up to 1 day in advance and refrigerated, tightly covered.

Turkey Burgers Provençal

Yield: 4–6 servings | Active time: 15 minutes | Start to finish: 45 minutes

1. Prepare a dual-temperature hot-and-medium grill according to the instructions given in Chapter 1.

2. Combine mayonnaise, basil, parsley, capers, garlic, shallot, herbes de Provence, salt, and pepper in a mixing bowl, and stir well.

3. Combine ½ cup mayonnaise mixture and turkey in a mixing bowl, and mix gently. Form mixture into 4–6 (¾-inch-thick) burgers.

4. Grill rolls on the hot side of the grill cut-side down until toasted. Sear burgers over high heat for 2 minutes per side, uncovered if using a charcoal grill, and then transfer burgers to the cooler side of the grill. Continue to cook, covered, for 3–5 minutes per side or until burgers register 160°F on an instant-read thermometer and are cooked through and no longer pink.

5. Serve immediately with remaining mayonnaise mixture, lettuce, tomato, and onion.

VARIATION: *Ground pork or ground veal can be substituted for the turkey. Cook these meats to desired doneness.*

Note: The turkey mixture can be prepared up to 1 day in advance and refrigerated, tightly covered.

1 cup mayonnaise

1 cup tightly packed chopped fresh basil

¼ cup chopped fresh parsley

¼ cup small capers, drained and rinsed

2 garlic cloves, peeled and minced

1 large shallot, peeled and chopped

2 teaspoons herbes de Provence

Salt and freshly ground black pepper to taste

1¾ pounds ground turkey

4–6 rolls of your choice, sliced in half

Lettuce, tomato, and thinly sliced red onion

1¾ pounds ground chuck

¾ cup grated cheddar cheese

2 garlic cloves, peeled and minced

1 tablespoon chopped fresh thyme or 1 teaspoon dried

Salt and freshly ground black pepper to taste

2 tablespoons unsalted butter

1 tablespoon olive oil

¼ pound fresh mushrooms, wiped with a damp paper towel, and sliced

4–6 rolls of your choice, sliced in half

4–6 slices cheddar cheese

Lettuce, tomato, and thinly sliced red onion

Fancy Cheese Burgers

Yield: 4–6 servings | Active time: 15 minutes | Start to finish: 40 minutes

1. Prepare a medium-hot grill according to the instructions given in Chapter 1.

2. Combine ground beef, cheddar cheese, garlic, thyme, salt, and pepper in a mixing bowl, and mix gently. Form mixture into 4–6 (1-inch-thick) burgers. Press with your thumb in the center of each burger to form an indentation; this keeps the burgers from creating a dome in the center.

3. Heat butter and oil in a large skillet over medium-high heat. Add mushrooms and cook, stirring frequently, for 4–5 minutes, or until mushrooms are brown. Season to taste with salt and pepper, and set aside.

4. Grill rolls cut-side down until toasted. Grill burgers beginning with the side with the indentation up, uncovered if using a charcoal grill, for a total time of 4–6 minutes per side or to an internal temperature of 125°F for medium-rare or to desired doneness. Top burgers with sliced cheese for the last two minutes of grilling. Serve immediately with sauteed mushrooms, lettuce, tomato, and onion.

VARIATION: *Ground turkey can be substituted for the beef. Cook turkey to an internal temperature of 160°F on an instant-read thermometer or until cooked through and no longer pink. Also, blue cheese can be substituted for the cheddar cheese.*

Note: The beef mixture can be prepared up to 1 day in advance and refrigerated, tightly covered.

Beef burger

Tex-Mex Beef and Chorizo Burgers

Yield: 4–6 servings | Active time: 15 minutes | Start to finish: 40 minutes

1. Prepare a medium-hot grill according to the instructions given in Chapter 1.

2. Remove casings from chorizo, if necessary, and chop chorizo finely in a food processor fitted with a steel blade, using on-and-off pulsing. Combine chorizo, ground chuck, shallots, 3 garlic cloves, cilantro, chili powder, cumin, and oregano in a mixing bowl. Season to taste with salt and cayenne. Mix well, and form mixture into 8–12 (⅓-inch-thick) patties. Place cheese on half of patties, and top with remaining patties. Press together gently to enclose cheese. Press with your thumb in the center of each burger to form an indentation; this keeps the burgers from creating a dome in the center.

3. Combine mayonnaise, remaining garlic, green chiles, and lime juice in a small bowl. Season with salt and cayenne to taste, and stir well. Set aside.

4. Grill rolls cut-side down until toasted. Grill burgers beginning with the side with the indentation up, uncovered if using a charcoal grill, for a total time of 4–6 minutes per side or to an internal temperature of 125°F for medium-rare or to desired doneness. To serve, place burgers on bottom half of rolls and top each with mayonnaise. Serve immediately with lettuce, tomato, and red onion.

VARIATION: *Ground turkey can be substituted for the beef. Cook burgers to an internal temperature of 160°F on an instant-read thermometer or until cooked through and no longer pink.*

Note: The beef mixture can be prepared up to 1 day in advance and refrigerated, tightly covered.

½ pound chorizo

1 pound ground chuck

2 shallots, peeled and finely chopped

4 garlic cloves, peeled and minced, divided

3 tablespoons chopped fresh cilantro

2 tablespoons chili powder

2 teaspoon ground cumin

1 teaspoon dried oregano

Salt and cayenne to taste

1 cup grated jalapeño Jack cheese

¾ cup mayonnaise

2 tablespoons diced canned, mild green chiles, drained

1 tablespoon freshly squeezed lime juice

4–6 rolls of your choice, sliced in half

Lettuce, tomato, and thinly sliced red onion

1¾ pounds ground pork

12 scallions, white parts and 2 inches of green tops, trimmed, and thinly sliced, divided

¼ cup grated fresh ginger

¼ cup chopped fresh cilantro

4 garlic cloves, peeled and minced

¼ cup soy sauce

2 tablespoons dry sherry

½ cup finely chopped water chestnuts

Freshly ground black pepper to taste

½ cup Dijon mustard

¼ cup hoisin sauce*

4–6 sesame rolls, sliced in half

Lettuce and tomato

* Available in the Asian aisle of most supermarkets and in specialty markets.

Chinese Pork Burgers

Yield: 4–6 servings | Active time: 20 minutes | Start to finish: 45 minutes

1. Prepare a medium-hot grill according to the instructions given in Chapter 1.

2. Combine pork, half of scallions, ginger, cilantro, garlic, soy sauce, sherry, water chestnuts, and pepper in a mixing bowl. Mix well and form into 4–6 (¾-inch-thick) burgers. Press with your thumb in the center of each burger to form an indentation; this keeps the burgers from creating a dome in the center.

3. Combine mustard and hoisin sauce in a bowl, whisk well, and set aside.

4. Grill rolls cut-side down until toasted. Grill burgers beginning with the side with the indentation up, uncovered if using a charcoal grill, for a total time of 4–6 minutes per side or to an internal temperature of 150˚F on an instant-read thermometer. Baste burgers with sauce for last 4 minutes of grilling.

5. Add remaining scallions to remaining basting sauce. Serve burgers immediately on rolls with lettuce and tomato. Pass sauce separately.

VARIATION: *Ground turkey or ground veal can be substituted for the pork. The turkey should be grilled to an internal temperature of 160˚F or until cooked through and no longer pink.*

Note: The pork mixture can be prepared up to 1 day in advance and refrigerated, tightly covered.

Chinese Pork Burger

Crunchy Southwestern Pork Burgers

Yield: 4–6 servings | Active time: 15 minutes | Start to finish: 40 minutes

1. Prepare a medium-hot grill according to the instructions given in Chapter 1.

2. Combine pork, crushed tortilla chips, onion, garlic, cilantro, chili powder, cumin, oregano, salt, and pepper in a mixing bowl. Mix well and form into 4–6 (¾-inch-thick) burgers. Press with your thumb in the center of each burger to form an indentation; this keeps the burgers from creating a dome in the center.

3. Grill rolls cut-side down until toasted. Grill burgers beginning with the side with the indentation up, uncovered if using a charcoal grill, for a total time of 4–6 minutes per side or to an internal temperature of 150°F on an instant-read thermometer. Serve immediately on rolls with lettuce and salsa.

VARIATION: *Ground turkey or ground veal can be substituted for the pork. The turkey should be grilled to an internal temperature of 160°F or until cooked through and no longer pink.*

Note: The pork mixture can be prepared up to 1 day in advance and refrigerated, tightly covered.

1¾ pounds ground pork

½ cup tortilla chips (crushed in heavy resealable plastic bag)

¼ cup finely chopped red onion

2 garlic cloves, peeled and minced

3 tablespoons chopped fresh cilantro

1 tablespoon chili powder

1 teaspoon ground cumin

½ teaspoon dried oregano

Salt and freshly ground black pepper to taste

4–6 rolls of your choice, sliced in half

Lettuce and chunky tomato salsa

Greek Lamb Burgers

Yield: 4–6 servings | Active time: 20 minutes | Start to finish: 40 minutes

1. Prepare a medium-hot grill according to the instructions given in Chapter 1.

2. Place yogurt in a strainer set over a mixing bowl. Shake strainer gently a few times, and allow yogurt to drain for at least 30 minutes at room temperature or up to 6 hours refrigerated. Discard whey from mixing bowl, and place yogurt in the bowl. Set aside.

3. Combine lamb, shallots, garlic, parsley, oregano, thyme, and cumin in a mixing bowl. Season to taste with salt and pepper. Mix well, and form mixture into 4–6 (1-inch-thick) burgers. Press with your thumb in the center of each burger to form an indentation; this keeps the burgers from creating a dome in the center.

4. Grill burgers beginning with the side with the indentation up, uncovered if using a charcoal grill, for a total time of 4–6 minutes per side or to an internal temperature of 125°F for medium-rare or to desired doneness. While burgers are grilling, combine drained yogurt, cucumber, and tomato in a small bowl. Season to taste with salt and pepper.

5. To serve, cut top 1 inch off pita breads and place burgers inside. Spoon yogurt mixture on top of each burger in pita bread, and serve immediately.

VARIATION: *Ground beef can be substituted for the ground lamb.*

Note: The lamb mixture can be prepared up to 1 day in advance and refrigerated, tightly covered.

⅔ cup plain yogurt

1¾ pounds ground lamb

2 shallots, peeled and finely chopped

3 garlic cloves, peeled and minced

¼ cup chopped fresh parsley

2 tablespoons chopped fresh oregano or 2 teaspoons dried

1 tablespoon chopped fresh thyme or 1 teaspoon dried

2 teaspoons ground cumin

Salt and freshly ground black pepper to taste

½ cup finely chopped cucumber

2 ripe plum tomatoes, cored, seeded, and finely chopped

4–6 (8-inch) pita breads

2 tablespoons vegetable oil

1 small onion, peeled and chopped

2 garlic cloves, peeled and minced

1 celery rib, rinsed, trimmed, and chopped

1 red bell pepper, seeds and ribs removed, and finely chopped

1½ pounds large (21–30 per pound) raw shrimp, peeled and deveined

3 tablespoons chopped fresh chives

3 tablespoons chopped fresh parsley

½ teaspoon hot red pepper sauce, or to taste

Cajun seasoning to taste

4–6 long submarine rolls, split in half

Lettuce, tomato, and tartar sauce

Shrimp Burgers

Yield: 4–6 servings | Active time: 20 minutes | Start to finish: 45 minutes

1. Prepare a dual-temperature hot-and-medium grill according to the instructions given in Chapter 1.

2. Heat oil in a large skillet over medium heat. Add onion, garlic, celery, and red bell pepper. Cook, stirring frequently, for 5–7 minutes or until vegetables are soft. Scrape mixture into a mixing bowl.

3. Finely chop ½ pound shrimp, and add to the bowl. Puree remaining 1 pound shrimp in a food processor fitted with a steel blade. Add to the bowl, along with chives, parsley, hot red pepper sauce, and Cajun seasoning. Form mixture into 8–12 oval (½-inch-thick) patties.

4. Grill rolls cut-side down until toasted. Sear shrimp burgers, uncovered if using a charcoal grill, for 2 minutes per side over hot heat, and then cook for an additional 2 minutes per side over medium heat or until cooked through. Serve immediately, placing 2 patties per person on rolls with lettuce, tomato, and tartar sauce.

VARIATION: *Scallops or a firm-fleshed white fish such as cod or tilapia can be substituted for the shrimp. Serve immediately on rolls with lettuce, tomato, and tartar sauce.*

Note: The shrimp mixture can be prepared up to 1 day in advance and refrigerated, tightly covered.

Middle Eastern Lentil Burgers

Yield: 4–6 servings | Active time: 20 minutes | Start to finish: 40 minutes

1. Place lentils in a 2-quart saucepan, cover with water and add 1 teaspoon salt. Bring to a boil over medium-high heat, then reduce the heat to low and simmer lentils, covered, for 20 to 25 minutes or until cooked. Drain lentils, and place in a mixing bowl.

2. Prepare a medium-hot grill according to the instructions given in Chapter 1.

3. While lentils simmer, place pine nuts in a small dry skillet over medium heat. Toast nuts, shaking pan frequently, for 2–3 minutes, or until browned. Remove nuts from the pan, and set aside. Heat oil in the same small skillet over medium-high heat. Add onions and garlic, and cook, stirring frequently, for 3 minutes, or until onion is translucent. Add coriander and cumin, and cook, stirring constantly, for 1 minute. Add onion mixture to lentils, and stir well.

4. Puree ½ cup pine nuts and 1 cup lentil mixture in a food processor fitted with a steel blade. Scrape mixture back into a mixing bowl, and add remaining lentil mixture and pine nuts. Season to taste with salt and pepper. Form mixture into 4–6 (¾-inch-thick) burgers.

5. Grill buns cut-side down until toasted. Grill burgers for 3 minutes per side, covered, turning them gently with a spatula. Serve immediately on buns with lettuce, tomato, and hummus.

Note: The lentil mixture can be prepared up to 1 day in advance and refrigerated, tightly covered. Allow it to reach room temperature before grilling the burgers.

2 cups lentils, picked over, rinsed, and drained

1 quart water

1 teaspoon salt

¾ cup pine nuts

2 tablespoons vegetable oil

1 medium onion, peeled and chopped

2 garlic cloves, peeled and minced

2 teaspoons ground coriander

1 teaspoon ground cumin

Salt and freshly ground black pepper to taste

6 sesame buns, sliced in half

Lettuce, tomato, and hummus

Chapter 11

Entree Salads

The recipes in this chapter can be considered a "two-fer." Entree salads—loaded with healthful fresh vegetables and some grilled protein—are also a great way to use up leftover grilled food from a previous meal. Stunning when they arrive at the table, the salads in this chapter are a complete meal, perhaps with the addition of some crusty bread. So do not be put off if the preparation time seems long; the salad is all you have to create.

1½ pounds boneless, skinless chicken breasts, rinsed and patted dry with paper towels

½ cup freshly squeezed lime juice

3 tablespoons chopped fresh cilantro

1 tablespoon dried oregano

3 garlic cloves, peeled and minced

Salt and freshly ground black pepper to taste

½ cup olive oil

2 teaspoons ground cumin

2 cups cooked corn kernels

1 (15-ounce) can black beans, drained and rinsed

1 large red bell pepper, seeds and ribs removed, and diced

3 scallions, white parts and 2 inches of green tops, trimmed and thinly sliced

6–8 cups bite-sized pieces romaine lettuce, rinsed and dried

Southwestern Grilled Chicken Salad

Yield: 6–8 servings | Active time: 25 minutes | Start to finish: 40 minutes

1. Prepare a hot grill according to the instructions given in Chapter 1.

2. Trim chicken breasts of all visible fat, and pound to an even thickness of ½ inch between two sheets of plastic wrap. Combine lime juice, cilantro, oregano, garlic, salt, and pepper in a jar with a tight-fitting lid, and shake well. Add olive oil, and shake well again.

3. Pour half of mixture into a heavy resealable plastic bag and add chicken. Marinate chicken at room temperature for 20 minutes, turning the bag occasionally. Add cumin to remaining dressing, and set aside.

4. Remove chicken from marinade, and discard marinade. Grill chicken for 2–3 minutes per side, uncovered, or until chicken is cooked through and no longer pink. Remove chicken from the grill, and cut into thin slices against the grain.

5. To serve, combine corn, beans, red pepper, and scallions in a mixing bowl, and toss with dressing. Mound greens onto a serving platter or individual plates, and top with vegetable mixture and chicken slices. Serve immediately, passing extra dressing separately.

VARIATION: *This salad is also excellent with grilled shrimp; consult a similar recipe for instructions on grilling the shrimp.*

Note: The dressing can be made up to 1 day in advance and refrigerated, tightly covered. Bring to room temperature before using.

Chicken and Spinach Salad

Yield: 6–8 servings | Active time: 25 minutes | Start to finish: 30 minutes

1. Prepare a hot grill according to the instructions given in Chapter 1.

2. Trim chicken breasts of all visible fat, and pound to an even thickness of ½ inch between two sheets of plastic wrap. Place chicken breasts in a mixing bowl, and toss with ¼ cup olive oil, garlic, sage, thyme, salt, and pepper.

3. Combine honey, mustard, vinegar, remaining ¾ cup oil, salt, and pepper in a mixing bowl, and whisk well. Set aside.

4. Grill chicken for 2–3 minutes per side, uncovered, or until chicken is cooked through and no longer pink. Remove chicken from the grill, and set aside.

5. To serve, combine spinach, carrots, bell pepper, and onion in a mixing bowl, and toss with enough dressing to coat vegetables lightly. Mound mixture onto a serving platter or individual plates, and top with chicken slices. Serve immediately, passing extra dressing separately.

VARIATION: *This salad is also excellent with grilled shrimp; consult a similar recipe for instructions on grilling the shrimp.*

Note: The dressing can be made up to 1 day in advance and refrigerated, tightly covered. Bring to room temperature before using.

1½ pounds boneless, skinless chicken breasts, rinsed and patted dry with paper towels

1 cup olive oil, divided

3 garlic cloves, peeled and minced

1 tablespoon dried sage

2 teaspoons dried thyme

Salt and freshly ground black pepper to taste

3 tablespoons honey

3 tablespoons Dijon mustard

⅓ cup cider vinegar

1½ pounds baby spinach, washed and stemmed if necessary

2 carrots, peeled and thinly sliced

1 red bell pepper, seeds and ribs removed, cut into thin slices

1 red onion, peeled and cut into thin rings

4 ripe plum tomatoes, rinsed, cored, seeded, and sliced

Chicken and Spinach Salad

1½ pounds boneless, skinless chicken breasts, rinsed and patted dry with paper towels

1 large egg

1 (2-ounce) tube anchovy paste

5 garlic cloves, peeled and minced

¼ cup freshly squeezed lemon juice

2 tablespoons Dijon mustard

½ cup extra-virgin olive oil, divided

Freshly ground black pepper to taste

6–8 (½-inch-thick) slices French or Italian bread

6–8 cups bite-sized pieces romaine lettuce, rinsed and dried

½ cup freshly grated Parmesan cheese

6–8 anchovy fillets (optional)

Grilled Chicken Caesar Salad

Yield: 6–8 servings | Active time: 25 minutes | Start to finish: 35 minutes

1. Prepare a hot grill according to the instructions given in Chapter 1.

2. Trim chicken breasts of all visible fat, and pound to an even thickness of ½ inch between two sheets of plastic wrap. Place chicken breasts in a mixing bowl.

3. To prepare dressing, bring a small saucepan of water to a boil over high heat. Add egg and boil for 1 minute. Remove egg from water with a slotted spoon and break it into a jar with a tight-fitting lid, scraping the inside of the shell. Add anchovy paste, garlic, lemon juice, and mustard, and shake well. Add ⅓ cup olive oil, and shake well again. Season to taste with pepper.

4. Reserve half of dressing, and mix remaining dressing into bowl with chicken breasts. Use reserved oil to brush both sides of bread.

5. Grill chicken for 2–3 minutes per side, uncovered, or until chicken is cooked through and no longer pink. Grill bread for 1–2 minutes per side, or until toasted. Remove chicken from the grill, and cut into thin slices against the grain. Remove bread from the grill, and cut into ½-inch croutons.

6. To serve, combine croutons, lettuce, and Parmesan in a mixing bowl, and toss with enough dressing to coat lightly. Mound mixture onto a serving platter or individual plates, and top with chicken slices and anchovies, if using. Serve immediately, passing extra dressing separately.

VARIATION: *Grilled shrimp or cubes of salmon can be used instead of chicken for an aquatic treat.*

Note: The dressing can be made up to 1 day in advance and refrigerated, tightly covered. Bring to room temperature before using.

Steak and Peach Salad

Yield: 4–6 servings | Active time: 25 minutes | Start to finish: 45 minutes

1. Prepare a dual-temperature hot-and-medium grill according to the instructions given in Chapter 1. Rinse steaks and pat dry with paper towels.

2. Combine chili powder, coriander, cumin, paprika, oregano, garlic powder, sugar, cinnamon, salt, and pepper in a small bowl, and stir well. Reserve 1 tablespoon of mixture, and rub remaining mixture onto all sides of steaks, and set aside. Combine reserved spice mix with brown sugar, and set aside.

3. Sear steaks on the hot side of the grill for 2–3 minutes per side, uncovered if using a charcoal grill, or until well browned. Transfer steaks to the cooler side of the grill, and cook for an additional 2–3 minutes per side, or until an instant-read thermometer registers 120°F, for rare. Remove steaks from the grill, and allow them to rest for 5 minutes.

4. Cut peaches in half, and discard stones. Rub brown sugar spice mixture on cut side. Grill peaches skin-side up for 4 minutes, uncovered if using a charcoal grill, then turn and grill skin-side down for an additional 3–4 minutes, or until peaches are tender.

5. Combine greens, scallions, red pepper, and red onion in a mixing bowl. To serve, toss salad with ⅓ cup of dressing. Mound mixture onto a serving platter or individual plates, and top with steak slices and peach halves. Serve immediately, passing extra dressing separately.

1½ pounds New York strip steak or boneless rib eye steak, at least 1 inch thick

1 tablespoon chili powder

1 tablespoon ground coriander

1 tablespoon ground cumin

1 tablespoon smoked Spanish paprika

1 tablespoon dried oregano

1 tablespoon garlic powder

1 teaspoon granulated sugar

¼ teaspoon ground cinnamon

Salt and freshly ground black pepper to taste

2 tablespoons firmly packed dark brown sugar

4–6 ripe peaches, unpeeled

4–6 cups baby salad greens, rinsed and dried

4 scallions, white parts and 2 inches of green tops, trimmed and sliced

½ red bell pepper, seeds and ribs removed, and thinly sliced

½ small red onion, peeled and thinly sliced

½ cup Hazelnut Vinaigrette (recipe on page 24)

1 (2-pound) flank steak

⅓ cup rice wine vinegar

3 tablespoons soy sauce

3 tablespoons Dijon
mustard

2 tablespoons hoisin sauce*

3 tablespoons grated fresh
ginger

4 garlic cloves, peeled and
minced

2 scallions, trimmed and
finely chopped

Freshly ground black
pepper to taste

¾ cup vegetable oil

¼ cup Asian sesame oil*

¼ pound snow peas, tips
removed

1 pound baby spinach
leaves, rinsed and
stemmed

¼ pound bean sprouts,
rinsed

2 cucumbers, peeled,
halved, and thinly sliced

1 red bell pepper, seeds
and ribs removed, thinly
sliced

* Available in the Asian aisle
of most supermarkets and in
specialty markets.

Asian Steak Salad

Yield: 6–8 servings | Active time: 25 minutes | Start to finish: 4¼ hours, including 4 hours for marinating

1. Rinse steak and pat dry with paper towels. Score steak with a paring knife on both sides in a diagonal pattern ¼ inch deep.

2. Combine vinegar, soy sauce, mustard, hoisin sauce, ginger, garlic, scallions, and pepper in a jar with a tight-fitting lid. Shake well. Add vegetable and sesame oils, and shake well again.

3. Place steak in a heavy resealable plastic bag, and add ½ cup of dressing. Marinate steak, refrigerated, for 4 hours, turning the bag occasionally.

4. While steak marinates, place snow peas in a microwave-safe container with 1 tablespoon water. Microwave on high (100% power) for 30 seconds. Plunge snow peas into a bowl of ice water. Drain. Combine snow peas with spinach, bean sprouts, cucumbers, and red pepper in a salad bowl, and refrigerate.

5. Prepare a hot grill according to the instructions given in Chapter 1.

6. Grill steak for 5–7 minutes, uncovered if using a charcoal grill, or until browned. Turn meat with tongs, and grill for an additional 2–3 minutes for medium-rare, or to desired doneness. Allow steak to rest for 5 minutes, then slice it thinly on the diagonal.

7. To serve, toss salad with ⅓ cup of dressing. Mound mixture onto a serving platter or individual plates, and top with steak slices. Serve immediately, passing extra dressing separately.

VARIATION: *You can substitute slices of grilled chicken breast or fish steaks for the beef in this recipe. Consult a similar recipe for cooking instructions.*

Note: The dressing can be made up to 1 day in advance and refrigerated, tightly covered. Bring to room temperature before using.

Steak and Blue Cheese Salad

Yield: 4–6 servings | Active time: 25 minutes | Start to finish: 45 minutes

1. Prepare a dual-temperature hot-and-medium grill according to the instructions given in Chapter 1.

2. Sprinkle steaks with salt and pepper. Combine vinegar, garlic, shallot, parsley, thyme, sugar, salt, and pepper in a jar with a tight-fitting lid, and shake well. Add olive oil, and shake well again. Set aside.

3. Sear steaks on the hot side of the grill for 2–3 minutes per side, uncovered if using a charcoal grill, or until well browned. Transfer steaks to the cooler side of the grill, and cook for an additional 2–3 minutes per side, or until an instant-read thermometer registers 120°F, for rare. Remove steaks from the grill, and allow them to rest for 5 minutes.

4. Combine romaine, radicchio, onion, tomatoes, and blue cheese in a mixing bowl. To serve, toss salad with ⅓ cup of dressing. Mound mixture onto a serving platter or individual plates, and top with steak slices. Serve immediately, passing extra dressing separately.

Note: The dressing can be made up to 1 day in advance and refrigerated, tightly covered. Bring to room temperature before using.

1½ pounds New York strip steak or boneless rib eye steak, at least 1 inch thick

Salt and freshly ground black pepper to taste

½ cup red wine vinegar

2 garlic cloves, peeled and minced

1 shallot, peeled and minced

2 tablespoons chopped fresh parsley

1 tablespoon chopped fresh thyme or 1 teaspoon dried

2 teaspoons granulated sugar

1 cup olive oil

4 cups bite-sized pieces romaine lettuce, rinsed and dried

1 large head radicchio, rinsed, cored, and chopped

½ small red onion, peeled and thinly sliced

4 small tomatoes, rinsed, cored, and cut into wedges

1 cup crumbled blue cheese

Steak and Blue Cheese Salad

79

1 cup cracked-wheat bulgur

2 cups boiling water

1 (15-ounce) can garbanzo beans, drained and rinsed

2 large tomatoes, cored, seeded, and diced

1 cup chopped fresh parsley

1 bunch scallions, white parts and 2 inches of green tops, rinsed, trimmed, and thinly sliced

½ cup freshly squeezed lemon juice

¼ cup chopped fresh mint

¼ cup olive oil

Salt and freshly ground black pepper to taste

1 (3-pound) butterflied boneless leg of lamb (see method in Chapter 9)

3–4 (12-inch) metal skewers

½ head romaine lettuce, rinsed and dried

Middle Eastern Lamb Salad

Yield: 6–8 servings | Active time: 25 minutes | Start to finish: 1¼ hours

1. Place bulgur in a large mixing bowl. Stir in boiling water, cover the bowl, and allow bulgur to stand for 1 hour. Add beans, tomatoes, parsley, scallions, lemon juice, mint, olive oil, salt, and pepper to bulgur, and mix well. Refrigerate salad, tightly covered.

2. Prepare a hot grill according to the instructions given in Chapter 1. Preheat the oven to 375°F.

3. Sprinkle lamb with salt and pepper. Spear lamb lengthwise through the thickest part of the meat with the skewers to keep it level. Sear lamb on hot grill, uncovered, for 4 minutes per side.

4. Remove lamb from the grill, and place lamb in a broiler pan. Roast lamb for 15–20 minutes, or until it registers 125°F on an instant-read thermometer for medium-rare. Remove lamb from the oven, and cover it loosely with foil. Allow lamb to rest for 10 minutes, then carve into slices across the grain.

5. To serve, line a platter or individual plates with lettuce leaves, and mound bulgur salad on top of lettuce. Top salad with lamb slices, and serve immediately.

Note: The lamb can be seared up to 4 hours in advance and kept at room temperature before roasting. The bulgur salad can be made up to 1 day in advance and refrigerated, tightly covered.

Tex-Mex Pork Salad

Yield: 4–6 servings | Active time: 20 minutes | Start to finish: 1 hour

1. Prepare a medium-hot grill according to the instructions given in Chapter 1. Rinse pork and pat dry with paper towels. Cut off all visible fat.

2. Combine orange juice, lime juice, vinegar, cilantro, garlic, chile, salt, and pepper in a jar with a tight-fitting lid, and shake well. Add olive oil, and shake well again. Pour half of dressing into a heavy resealable plastic bag, and add chili powder and cumin. Mix well. Add pork, and marinate at room temperature for 20 minutes, turning the bag occasionally.

3. Remove pork from marinade, and discard marinade. Grill pork for 3–4 minutes per side, or until cooked through. Brush vegetables with dressing. Grill pepper sections and onion slices for 4–5 minutes per side. Allow pork to rest for 5 minutes.

4. Cut peppers into strips, and separate onion slices into rings. Slice pork thinly against the grain.

5. Combine lettuce and tomato in a large mixing bowl. Toss salad with half of remaining dressing. Mound mixture onto a serving platter or individual plates, and top with pork, pepper, and onion slices. Sprinkle broken tortilla chips over all, and serve immediately, passing extra dressing separately.

VARIATION: *Boneless, skinless chicken breasts also work well in this recipe; consult a similar recipe for instructions on how to cook the chicken.*

Note: The dressing can be made up to 1 day in advance and refrigerated, tightly covered. Bring to room temperature before using.

- 1½ pounds boneless pork chops
- 3 tablespoons freshly squeezed orange juice
- 3 tablespoons freshly squeezed lime juice
- 1 tablespoon sherry vinegar
- 2 tablespoons chopped fresh cilantro
- 2 garlic cloves, peeled and minced
- 1 small jalapeño or serrano chile, seeds and ribs removed, and finely chopped
- Salt and freshly ground black pepper to taste
- ½ cup extra-virgin olive oil
- 2 tablespoons chili powder
- 1 tablespoon ground cumin
- 2 red bell peppers, seeds and ribs removed, and quartered lengthwise
- 1 large red onion, peeled and cut into ½-inch slices
- 4 cups bite-sized pieces romaine lettuce, rinsed and dried
- 2 large tomatoes, cored, seeded, and diced
- 2 cups broken tortilla chips

8–12 (8-inch) bamboo skewers

⅓ cup freshly squeezed lemon juice

4 garlic cloves, peeled and minced

2 tablespoons chopped fresh oregano or 2 teaspoons dried

2 tablespoons chopped fresh parsley

Salt and freshly ground black pepper to taste

½ cup extra-virgin olive oil, divided

1 pint cherry tomatoes, rinsed and halved

½ English cucumber, cut into ⅓-inch dice

½ small red onion, peeled, halved lengthwise, and thinly sliced

1½ pounds extra large (16–20 per pound) raw shrimp, peeled and deveined

1 orange or yellow bell pepper, seeds and ribs removed, and cut into ½-inch slices

4–6 cups chopped romaine

1 cup crumbled feta cheese

1 cup pitted kalamata olives

Greek Shrimp Salad

Yield: 4–6 servings | Active time: 20 minutes | Start to finish: 40 minutes

1. Soak bamboo skewers in warm water to cover, and prepare a medium-hot grill according to the instructions given in Chapter 1.

2. Combine lemon juice, garlic, oregano, parsley, salt, and pepper in a jar with a tight-fitting lid, and shake well. Add ⅓ cup olive oil, and shake well again.

3. Place tomatoes, cucumber, and red onion in a large mixing bowl. Toss with one-third of dressing, and refrigerate. Place shrimp in a heavy resealable plastic bag, and add one-third of dressing. Seal and turn bag to coat shrimp evenly. Marinate shrimp at room temperature for 10 minutes, or up to 30 minutes refrigerated.

4. Grill pepper slices, covered, for 3–5 minutes, or until soft. Remove peppers from the grill, and slice into strips. Add peppers to bowl with other vegetables.

5. Remove shrimp from marinade, and discard marinade. Divide shrimp into 4–6 groups, and thread each group onto two parallel skewers. Grill shrimp, covered, for 2 minutes per side, or until pink and cooked through. Remove shrimp from skewers.

6. To serve, place 1 portion lettuce on each plate, and top with vegetables and shrimp. Sprinkle feta and olives on top, and serve immediately, passing remaining dressing separately.

VARIATION: *Any firm white-fleshed fish fillet, such as halibut or cod, will be just as delicious as the shrimp and will cook in the same amount of time. You can also substitute ¾-inch cubes of boneless, skinless chicken breast. The chicken should be marinated in the refrigerator for 1 hour, and the pieces should be cooked for 4–6 minutes per side, or until cooked through and no longer pink.*

Note: The dressing can be made up to 1 day in advance and refrigerated, tightly covered. Bring to room temperature before using.

Chapter 12

Combination Cooking

This chapter is not one you will find in many cookbooks on grilling; it is the result of literally decades of experimentation as I have tried to push the limits of what can be cooked on a grill and how to give food the best flavor. All of the recipes in this chapter start on the grill; they are then finished in a conventional oven. Some recipes are then roasted in a relatively cool oven to complete cooking, while others begin by being seared or smoked on the grill and are then braised to that wonderful term—fork tender.

Aromatic Roast Chicken

Timing Rolled Roasts

Roasts cook more evenly if they are boned and rolled rather than left on the bone. While bones help retain moisture, the meat next to bones does not cook at the same rate since the bones act as insulation against the air carrying the heat. When tied, the string should be firm enough to hold the meat together in a neat cylinder, but should not be so tight as to be pressing into the flesh so that the exterior of the roast is bumpy. When the tissue is compressed at the points where the strings are tied, those portions of meat will cook at a slower rate, so the interior will not be evenly cooked.

Here is a chart of the general temperatures to which meats are roasted:

Roasting Temperature for Meat	
MEAT	DESIRED INTERNAL TEMPERATURE
Beef and Lamb	120°F—Rare 125°F–130°F—Medium Rare 135°F—Medium
Pork	145°F–150°F
Veal	150°F–155°F

While most cookbooks calculate roasting times in an equation of minutes per pound, I have a different method. I roast meats by the circumference. A 3-pound boneless pork loin can be short and squat, or it can be long and thin.

The easiest way to determine the circumference of a roast is with a tape measure. Stand the roast on its end, and place the tape measure snugly around what would be the waistline. Here is a chart to help you judge when to start taking the temperature of different roasts:

Roasting Times for Meat

These are total times for boneless roasts, with the initial searing taking place on the grill, and then the meat roasted in a 350°F oven for the remainder of the cooking time.

CIRCUMFERENCE	BEEF/LAMB (125°F)	VEAL (150°F)	PORK (150°F)
9 inches	30–35 min.	50–55 min.	55–60 min.
10 inches	35–45 min.	55–65 min.	60–70 min.
11 inches	45–50 min.	65–70 min.	75–85 min.
12 inches	55–60 min.	70–75 min.	85–95 min.
13 inches	60–65 min.	75–85 min.	95–105 min.
14 inches	70–75 min.	85–95 min.	105–115 min.
15 inches	75–80 min.	95–110 min.	115–125 min.
16 inches	80–90 min.	110–115 min.	125–130 min.

Smoked Beef Brisket

Yield: 8–10 servings | Active time: 20 minutes | Start to finish: 3½ hours

2 cups mesquite chips
1 (4–5-pound) beef brisket
3 tablespoons yellow mustard
Salt and freshly ground black pepper to taste
6 garlic cloves, peeled and minced
½ cup paprika
¼ cup firmly packed dark brown sugar
2 tablespoons chipotle chile powder
3 cups beef stock

1. Prepare a medium-hot grill according to the instructions given in Chapter 1. If using a charcoal grill, soak mesquite chips in water for 30 minutes. If using a gas grill, create a packet for wood chips as described in Chapter 1.

2. Rinse brisket and pat dry with paper towels. Rub brisket with mustard, and season to taste with salt and pepper. Combine garlic, paprika, brown sugar, and chipotle powder in a small bowl, and rub mixture all over brisket.

3. Preheat the oven to 350°F. Place wood chips on the grill. Sear brisket, covered, for a total of 20 minutes, turning with tongs after 10 minutes. Transfer brisket to a roasting pan, and add stock. Bring to a boil on top of the stove, then transfer to the oven, and bake for 2–2½ hours, covered, or until fork tender.

4. Remove brisket to a warm platter and tip the roasting pan to spoon off as much grease as possible. Slice brisket against the grain into thin slices. Spoon some pan juices over meat.

VARIATION: *You can also use this recipe for a boneless pork shoulder; the cooking time will be reduced to 1½–2 hours.*

Note: The brisket can be prepared up to 2 days in advance and refrigerated. If cooked in advance, remove the layer of grease, which will have hardened on the top. Reheat, covered, in a 350°F oven for 25–35 minutes, or until hot.

1 cup mesquite chips

6 (1-pound) lamb shanks

Salt and freshly ground
   black pepper to taste

⅓ cup olive oil

2 medium onions, peeled
   and diced

2 celery ribs, rinsed,
   trimmed, and diced

2 carrots, peeled, trimmed,
   and sliced

4 garlic cloves, peeled and
   minced

2 tablespoons chopped
   fresh parsley

1 tablespoon chopped
   fresh rosemary or 1
   teaspoon dried

1 tablespoon chopped
   fresh oregano or 1
   teaspoon dried

2 teaspoons chopped fresh
   thyme or ½ teaspoon
   dried

2 tablespoons tomato
   paste

1½ cups Barolo, or other
   dry red wine

1 cup beef stock

1 tablespoon cornstarch

2 tablespoons cold water

Braised Lamb Shanks

Yield: 6 servings | Active time: 20 minutes | Start to finish: 3 hours

1. Prepare a medium-hot grill according to the instructions given in Chapter 1. If using a charcoal grill, soak mesquite chips in water for 30 minutes. If using a gas grill, create a packet for wood chips as described in Chapter 1.

2. Wipe lamb shanks well with a damp cloth and remove any fat. Season with salt and pepper, and set aside.

3. While grill heats, heat oil in a Dutch oven over medium-high heat. Add onions, celery, carrots, and garlic, and cook, stirring frequently, for 3 minutes, or until onions are translucent.

4. Preheat the oven to 350°F. Place mesquite chips on the grill. Sear lamb shanks for a total of 15 minutes, covered, turning shanks with tongs to sear all sides.

5. Transfer shanks to the Dutch oven, and add parsley, rosemary, oregano, thyme, tomato paste, wine, and stock. Bring to a boil on top of the stove, then transfer to the oven, and bake for 1½–2 hours, or until fork tender.

6. Remove shanks to a warm platter and tip the Dutch oven to spoon off as much grease as possible. Cook sauce over medium heat until reduced by half. Mix cornstarch and water in a small cup, and add to sauce. Simmer for 3 minutes or until slightly thickened. Season sauce to taste with salt and pepper, then pour sauce over shanks, and serve immediately.

Note: The shanks can be prepared up to 3 days in advance and refrigerated. If cooked in advance, remove the layer of grease, which will have hardened on the top. Reheat, covered, in a 350°F oven for 25–35 minutes, or until hot.

Braised Lamb Shanks

Pulled Pork Barbecue

Yield: 10–12 servings | Active time: 20 minutes | Start to finish: 9 hours, including 6 hours for marinating

1. Rinse pork and pat dry with paper towels. Combine vegetable oil, garlic, onion, paprika, sugar, mustard, salt, and pepper in a small bowl. Rub paste all over pork, and refrigerate pork for a minimum of 6 hours or up to 24 hours, tightly covered with plastic wrap.

2. Prepare a medium-hot grill according to the instructions given in Chapter 1. If using a charcoal grill, soak hickory chips in water for 30 minutes. If using a gas grill, create a packet for wood chips as described in Chapter 1.

3. Preheat the oven to 350°F. Place wood chips on the grill. Sear pork, covered, for a total of 25 minutes, turning with tongs to sear all sides. Remove pork from the grill, and cut into 2-inch cubes.

4. Transfer pork cubes to a roasting pan, and add stock. Bring to a boil on top of the stove, then transfer to the oven, and bake for 2–2½ hours, covered, or until fork tender.

5. Using two forks, shred pork into bite-sized pieces. Mix meat with My Favorite Barbecue Sauce. To serve, mound meat onto buns, and top with coleslaw. Serve immediately.

Note: The meat can be prepared up to 3 days in advance and refrigerated, tightly covered. Reheat, covered with foil, in a 350°F oven for 20–30 minutes, or until hot.

1 (6–8-pound) boneless Boston pork butt, cut into quarters

¼ cup vegetable oil

4 garlic cloves, peeled and minced

1 small onion, peeled and chopped

2 tablespoons paprika

2 tablespoons firmly packed light brown sugar

1 tablespoon dry mustard

Salt and freshly ground black pepper to taste

3 cups hickory chips

3 cups chicken stock or pork stock

My Favorite Barbecue Sauce (recipe on page 20)

10–12 hamburger buns

2–3 cups coleslaw

2 cups hickory or apple wood chips

1 (3-pound) boneless center-cut pork loin roast

5 garlic cloves, peeled and minced, divided

2 tablespoons dried sage

1 tablespoon dried thyme

½ teaspoon ground allspice

Salt and freshly ground black pepper to taste

3 large tomatoes, cut in half

1 large onion, cut in half

1 Granny Smith apple, peeled, cored, and quartered

½ cup granulated sugar

½ cup cider vinegar

¼ cup golden raisins

2 tablespoons grated fresh ginger

¼ teaspoon cayenne

Pork Loin with Smoked Apple Chutney

Yield: 6–8 servings | Active time: 25 minutes | Start to finish: 1¾ hours

1. Prepare a hot grill according to the instructions given in Chapter 1. If using a charcoal grill, soak hickory or apple wood chips in water for 30 minutes. If using a gas grill, create a packet for wood chips as described in Chapter 1.

2. Rinse pork and pat dry with paper towels. Combine 3 garlic cloves, sage, thyme, allspice, salt, and pepper in a small bowl. Rub mixture into surfaces of pork.

3. Preheat the oven to 350°F. Place wood chips on the grill. Sear pork for a total of 10 minutes, covered, turning with tongs to sear all sides. Remove pork from the grill and place in a roasting pan.

4. Roast pork, uncovered, for 45–60 minutes, or until the temperature registers 145°F on an instant-read thermometer. The roasting time will depend on the thickness of the meat; consult the chart at the beginning of this chapter.

5. While pork roasts, prepare chutney. Cover the grill with a small-holed fish grill and place tomatoes, onion, and apple on the grill. Cover the grill with a lid and smoke vegetables and apple for 10 minutes. Remove vegetables and apple from the grill. Peel, core, and seed tomatoes. Peel and finely dice onion and apples. Place them in a large saucepan and add remaining garlic, sugar, vinegar, raisins, ginger, and cayenne.

6. Bring chutney to a boil over medium heat. Simmer, uncovered, for 30 minutes, or until thick, stirring occasionally.

7. Remove pork from the oven and place it on a platter, loosely covered with aluminum foil. Allow pork to rest for 15 minutes to allow juices to be reabsorbed into meat. Then slice thinly against the grain. Serve immediately, and pass chutney separately.

Note: The roast can be seared up to 3 hours in advance of roasting it; keep it at room temperature, lightly covered.

Aromatic Roast Chicken
Yield: 4 servings | Active time: 15 minutes | Start to finish: 2 hours

1 cup mesquite, hickory, or apple wood chips

1 (3½–4-pound) whole chicken, giblets removed

4 sprigs fresh parsley, divided

4 sprigs fresh rosemary, divided

6 garlic cloves, peeled, divided

1 orange, quartered

Salt and freshly ground black pepper to taste

4 tablespoons (½ stick) unsalted butter, softened

1 small onion, peeled and roughly chopped

1 carrot, peeled and thickly sliced

1 celery rib, rinsed, trimmed, and roughly chopped

1½ cups chicken stock, divided

1. Prepare a medium-hot grill according to the instructions given in Chapter 1. If using a charcoal grill, soak wood chips in water for 30 minutes. If using a gas grill, create a packet for wood chips as described in Chapter 1.

2. Rinse chicken, and pat dry with paper towels. Place 2 sprigs each of parsley and rosemary, 3 garlic cloves, and orange quarters in cavity of chicken. Sprinkle salt and pepper inside cavity, and close cavity with skewers.

3. Chop remaining parsley, rosemary, and garlic, and mix with butter. Season to taste with salt and pepper. Gently stuff mixture under skin of breast meat. Rub skin with salt and pepper. Truss chicken, if desired.

4. Preheat the oven to 350°F. Place wood chips on the grill. Sear chicken for a total of 15 minutes, covered, turning with tongs to brown all sides. Remove chicken from the grill, and place in a roasting pan, breast-side up.

5. Add onion, carrot, celery, and ½ cup chicken stock to the roasting pan. Cook an additional 1–1¼ hours, or until the juices run clear and the temperature of the dark meat registers 180°F on an instant-read thermometer. Remove chicken from the oven, and allow it to rest for 10 minutes, lightly covered.

6. Spoon all grease out of the pan, and add remaining chicken stock to the pan. Stir over medium-high heat until liquid is reduced to a syrupy consistency. Strain sauce into a sauce boat, and add to it any liquid that accumulates on the platter when chicken is carved. Carve chicken, and serve immediately.

VARIATION: *Tarragon can be substituted for the rosemary and parsley, and white wine can be used instead of chicken stock.*

Note: The chicken can be prepared for searing and roasting up to 6 hours in advance and refrigerated, tightly covered.

Chapter 13

Pizzas

Cooking thin-crust pizzas on the grill is now all the rage, and they can be topped with myriad ingredients. The key to a successful grilled pizza is that it must be small; it is impossible to flip a large round on the grill, and it is essential to grill both sides of the dough. I usually make pizzas in two batches, and cut up the first batch to allow diners to start munching while the second batch cooks. If your grill is large enough to accommodate all four circles at once, go ahead and cook them simultaneously.

For an easy alternative to making pizza dough, in almost all cities you can now purchase ready-to-bake balls of pizza dough in the refrigerated dairy case. With a few balls of pizza dough handy, any pizza can be on the table in less time than it takes to have one delivered!

---

3 cups all-purpose flour, plus extra for working dough

1 package dry or fresh active yeast

1 teaspoon salt

1 tablespoon honey

2 tablespoons olive oil

¾ cup water

Basic Pizza Dough and Procedure

Yield: 4 (8-inch) pizzas | Active time: 15 minutes | Start to finish: 50 minutes, including 30 minutes for rising

1. Place flour and yeast in a mixing bowl or the bowl of an electric mixer fitted with a dough hook. Add salt, honey, olive oil, and water. Mix well until the dough forms a soft ball.

2. Transfer dough to a lightly floured surface and knead for 5 minutes or until smooth. Place dough in a greased deep mixing bowl and allow dough to rest, covered with a clean dry towel, for 30 minutes.

3. Divide dough into 4 equal parts, and roll each piece into a smooth, tight ball. Place balls on a flat dish, covered with a damp towel, and refrigerate until grilling time. (This can be done up to 6 hours in advance, but dough should be removed from the refrigerator 1 hour before grilling to reach room temperature.)

4. Lightly flour a work surface, and using the fleshy part of your fingertips, flatten each dough ball into a circle approximately 6 inches in diameter, leaving outer edge thicker than center. Dust dough on both sides with flour. Lift dough from the work surface and gently stretch the edges, working clockwise, to form dough circles that are ¼ inch thick. Sprinkle additional flour on pizza paddles or baking sheets, and place pizza circles on top of flour. Lightly rub a long sheet of plastic wrap with flour, then invert loosely over pizza rounds and let them stand to puff slightly while preparing the grill, 10 to 20 minutes.

VARIATIONS: *Feel free to add a few tablespoons of chopped fresh herbs such as basil, oregano, or parsley to the basic pizza dough.*

Chorizo and Goat Cheese Pizza
Yield: 4 servings | Active time: 25 minutes | Start to finish: 50 minutes

1. Prepare a medium-hot grill according to the instructions given in Chapter 1. Shape pizza dough into 4 individual ¼-inch-thick rounds as described above in the recipe for Basic Pizza Dough.

2. Place chorizo in a skillet over medium-high heat, and cook, breaking up lumps with a fork, for 5–7 minutes, or until sausage is browned. Remove sausage from the pan with a slotted spoon, and drain on paper towels. Combine arugula and goat cheese in a small bowl, and season to taste with salt and pepper. Combine olive oil and garlic in a small bowl, and stir well.

3. Brush dough rounds with seasoned olive oil. Gently flip 2 dough rounds onto the grill, oiled-side down. Grill, uncovered, for 1½–2 minutes, or until grill marks form; burst bubbles that may appear on the surface with a long-handled meat fork. Brush tops with olive oil, and invert pizzas onto a baking sheet with the grilled side up.

4. Spread cheese mixture on pizzas, stopping ½ inch from the edge. Top with chorizo and peppers.

5. Return pizzas to the grill, and cover with pie tins. Grill, covered, for 1½–2 minutes, or until browned and cheese has melted. Serve immediately, and repeat with remaining 2 pizza rounds.

1 recipe Basic Pizza Dough or purchased pizza dough

½ pound fresh chorizo sausage, casings removed if necessary

1 cup firmly packed arugula leaves, rinsed and dried

10 ounces soft fresh goat cheese, crumbled

Salt and freshly ground black pepper to taste

3 tablespoons olive oil

2 garlic cloves, peeled and pressed through a garlic press

¼ red bell pepper, seeds and ribs removed, and chopped

¼ orange bell pepper, seeds and ribs removed, and chopped

2 (10-inch) aluminum pie tins

1 recipe Basic Pizza Dough or purchased pizza dough

1⅓ cups grated Monterey Jack cheese

1 tablespoon ground cumin

3 tablespoons olive oil

Salt and freshly ground black pepper to taste

1⅓ cups shredded cooked chicken

½ cup thinly sliced red onion

½ cup cooked corn kernels

¼ cup chopped fresh cilantro

2 jalapeño or serrano chiles, seeds and ribs removed, and finely chopped

2 (10-inch) aluminum pie tins

⅔ cup Summer Tomato Salsa (recipe on page 102) or purchased refrigerated salsa, drained

Southwestern Chicken Pizza

Yield: 4 servings | Active time: 20 minutes | Start to finish: 30 minutes

1. Prepare a medium-hot grill according to the instructions given in Chapter 1. Shape pizza dough into 4 individual ¼-inch-thick rounds as described above in the recipe for Basic Pizza Dough.

2. Mix cheese with cumin, and set aside. Brush dough rounds with olive oil, and sprinkle with salt and pepper. Gently flip 2 dough rounds onto the grill, oiled-side down. Grill, uncovered, for 1½–2 minutes, or until grill marks form; burst bubbles that may appear on the surface with a long-handled meat fork. Brush tops with olive oil, and invert pizzas onto a baking sheet with the grilled side up.

3. Cover crusts with cheese, chicken, onion, corn, cilantro, and chiles, stopping ½ inch from the edge. Season to taste with salt and pepper.

4. Return pizzas to the grill, and cover with pie tins. Grill, covered, for 1½–2 minutes, or until browned and cheese has melted. Serve immediately, garnished with salsa, and repeat with remaining 2 pizza rounds.

1 recipe Basic Pizza Dough or purchased pizza dough

½ cup olive oil, divided

2 red bell peppers, seeds and ribs removed, and thinly sliced

1 tablespoon crushed red pepper flakes

¾ pound fresh whole-milk mozzarella cheese, grated

¼ pound fontina cheese, grated

Salt and freshly ground black pepper to taste

½ cup chopped fresh basil

4 ripe plum tomatoes, rinsed, cored, seeded, and thinly sliced

6 ounces prosciutto, cut into fine julienne strips

4 scallions, white parts and 2 inches of green tops, trimmed and thinly sliced

4 ounces fresh goat cheese, crumbled

2 (10-inch) aluminum pie tins

Prosciutto Pizza

Yield: 4 servings | Active time: 15 minutes | Start to finish: 35 minutes

1. Prepare a medium-hot grill according to the instructions given in Chapter 1. Shape pizza dough into 4 individual ¼-inch-thick rounds as described above in the recipe for Basic Pizza Dough.

2. Heat ¼ cup olive oil in a large skillet over medium-high heat. Add red bell peppers and cook, stirring frequently, for 5 minutes, or until peppers are soft. Mix remaining ¼ cup oil with crushed red pepper, and set aside. Combine mozzarella and fontina cheeses, and set aside.

3. Brush dough rounds with seasoned olive oil, and sprinkle with salt and pepper. Gently flip 2 dough rounds onto the grill, oiled-side down. Grill, uncovered, for 1½–2 minutes, or until grill marks form; burst bubbles that may appear on the surface with a long-handled meat fork. Brush tops with olive oil, and invert pizzas onto a baking sheet with the grilled side up.

4. Spread mixed cheeses on top, reserving 1 cup cheese, stopping ½ inch from the edge. Sprinkle with basil and top with tomatoes, prosciutto, red peppers, and scallions. Dot with goat cheese, and finish by sprinkling with reserved cheese.

5. Return pizzas to the grill, and cover with pie tins. Grill, covered, for 1½–2 minutes, or until browned and cheese has melted. Serve immediately, and repeat with remaining 2 pizza rounds.

Pizza Margherita

Yield: 4 servings | Active time: 20 minutes | Start to finish: 30 minutes

1. Prepare a medium-hot grill according to the instructions given in Chapter 1. Shape pizza dough into 4 individual ¼-inch-thick rounds as described above in the recipe for Basic Pizza Dough.

2. Place tomatoes in a sieve set over a mixing bowl to drain. Brush dough rounds with olive oil, and sprinkle with salt and pepper. Gently flip 2 dough rounds onto the grill, oiled-side down. Grill, uncovered, for 1½–2 minutes, or until grill marks form; burst bubbles that may appear on the surface with a long-handled meat fork. Brush tops with olive oil, and invert pizzas onto a baking sheet with the grilled side up.

3. Cover crusts with mozzarella, Parmesan, and then tomatoes, stopping ½ inch from the edge. Scatter basil over the top. Season to taste with salt and pepper, and drizzle with more olive oil.

4. Return pizzas to the grill, and cover with pie tins. Grill, covered, for 1½–2 minutes, or until browned and cheese has melted. Serve immediately, and repeat with remaining 2 pizza rounds.

VARIATION: *While it is not authentic, either fresh oregano or fresh chopped rosemary can be substituted for the basil.*

1 recipe Basic Pizza Dough or purchased pizza dough

8 ripe plum tomatoes, rinsed, cored, seeded, and chopped

¼ cup extra-virgin olive oil, divided

Salt and freshly ground black pepper to taste

½ pound whole-milk mozzarella cheese, thinly sliced

½ cup firmly packed chopped fresh basil leaves

¼ cup freshly grated Parmesan cheese

2 (10-inch) aluminum pie tins

Pizza Margherita

1 recipe Basic Pizza Dough
or purchased pizza dough

¼ pound smoked bacon

¼ cup extra-virgin olive oil

Salt and freshly ground
pepper to taste

3 cups grated cheddar
cheese

4 ripe plum tomatoes,
rinsed, cored, seeded, and
thinly sliced

1 cup sliced mushrooms

2 (10-inch) aluminum pie
tins

Bacon, Tomato, Mushroom, and Cheddar Pizza

Yield: 4 servings | Active time: 15 minutes | Start to finish: 35 minutes

1. Prepare a medium-hot grill according to the instructions given in Chapter 1. Shape pizza dough into 4 individual ¼-inch-thick rounds as described above in the recipe for Basic Pizza Dough.

2. Place bacon slices in a heavy skillet, and cook over medium-high heat, turning pieces as necessary, until bacon is crisp. Remove bacon with tongs, and drain on paper towels. When cool, crumble bacon, and set aside.

3. Brush dough rounds with olive oil, and sprinkle with salt and pepper. Gently flip 2 dough rounds onto the grill, oiled-side down. Grill, uncovered, for 1½–2 minutes, or until grill marks form; burst bubbles that may appear on the surface with a long-handled meat fork. Brush tops with olive oil, and invert pizzas onto a baking sheet with the grilled side up.

4. Cover crusts with cheddar, then tomatoes and mushrooms, stopping ½ inch from the edge. Scatter bacon over the top. Season to taste with salt and pepper.

5. Return pizzas to the grill, and cover with pie tins. Grill, covered, for 1½–2 minutes, or until browned and cheese has melted. Serve immediately, and repeat with remaining 2 pizza rounds.

**Bacon, Tomato, Mushroom, and
Cheddar Pizza**

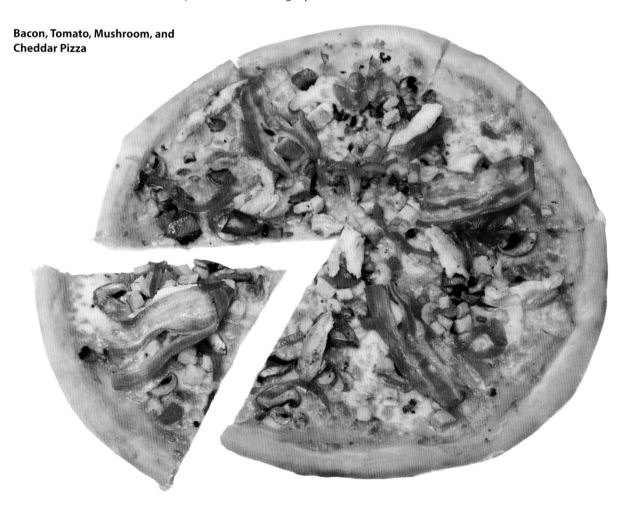

Greek-Style Pita Pizzas

Yield: 4 servings | Active time: 10 minutes | Start to finish: 35 minutes

1. Prepare a medium-hot grill according to the instructions given in Chapter 1. Combine tomatoes, olives, onion, 2 tablespoons olive oil, oregano, salt, and pepper in a mixing bowl. Mix well.

2. Brush pita breads with olive oil, and sprinkle with salt and pepper. Gently flip 2 pita breads onto the grill, oiled-side down. Grill, uncovered, for 1½–2 minutes, or until grill marks form. Brush tops with olive oil, and invert pitas onto a baking sheet with the grilled side up.

3. Cover crusts with vegetable mixture, stopping ½ inch from the edge. Scatter feta over the top. Season to taste with salt and pepper.

4. Return pizzas to the grill, and cover with pie tins. Grill, covered, for 1½–2 minutes, or until browned and cheese has melted. Repeat with remaining 2 pita breads. Serve immediately.

4 ripe plum tomatoes, rinsed, cored, seeded, and diced

½ cup chopped pitted kalamata olives

¼ cup chopped red onion

4 tablespoons olive oil, divided

2 tablespoons chopped fresh oregano or 2 teaspoons dried

Salt and freshly ground black pepper to taste

4 (8-inch) whole-wheat pita breads

½ cup crumbled feta cheese

2 (10-inch) aluminum pie tins

Chapter 14

Vegetables

It is only in recent decades that Americans have come to appreciate the wonderful flavors and textures that result from grilling vegetables. Cooking vegetables over high heat evaporates some of the high water content, and, therefore, intensifies the natural, sweet flavor.

Grilling accentuates vegetables' natural sugars.

Grilled Asparagus

Yield: 4–6 servings | Active time: 10 minutes | Start to finish: 30 minutes

	10 (8-inch) bamboo skewers
	2 pounds medium asparagus
	3 tablespoons olive oil
	Salt and freshly ground black pepper to taste

1. Soak bamboo skewers in warm water to cover, and prepare a medium-hot grill according to the instructions given in Chapter 1.

2. Break off woody ends from asparagus, and soak asparagus in water to cover for 10 minutes; rub the tips to dislodge any lingering grit.

3. Divide asparagus into groups, and thread them horizontally with 2 skewers per bunch into loose groups; do not push them together too tightly. Brush asparagus with oil, and sprinkle with salt and pepper.

4. Grill asparagus, covered, for 3–4 minutes per side, turning bunches with tongs. Serve immediately.

Southwest-Style Corn

Yield: 6 servings | Active time: 15 minutes | Start to finish: 35 minutes

	6 ears fresh corn
	Kitchen twine
	4 tablespoons (½ stick) unsalted butter
	2 tablespoons freshly squeezed lime juice
	1 tablespoon chili powder or to taste
	Salt and freshly ground black pepper to taste
	1 cup finely grated Monterey Jack or mild feta cheese
	2 tablespoons chopped fresh cilantro

1. Prepare a medium-hot grill according to the instructions given in Chapter 1.

2. Break stem end off corn, and discard all but one layer of husks. Pull back remaining husks, and pull off as much corn silk as possible. Draw husks back over kernels, and tie husks with kitchen twine. Soak corn in cold water to cover for 10 minutes.

3. Melt butter in a small saucepan over low heat. Stir in lime juice, chili powder, salt, and pepper. Combine cheese and cilantro on a plate.

4. Grill corn, uncovered if using a charcoal grill, for a total of 8–10 minutes, turning it with tongs every 1½–2 minutes. Corn is done when husks are charred and outline of kernels is visible.

5. Remove corn from the grill, and when cool enough to handle, remove and discard husks and any remaining corn silks. To serve, brush corn with butter mixture, and then roll in cheese. Serve immediately.

4–6 ears fresh corn

Kitchen twine

3 tablespoons unsalted butter, melted

Salt and freshly ground black pepper to taste

Grilled Corn

Yield: 4–6 servings | Active time: 10 minutes | Start to finish: 35 minutes

1. Prepare a medium-hot grill according to the instructions given in Chapter 1.

2. Break stem end off corn, and discard all but one layer of husks. Pull back remaining husks, and pull off as much corn silk as possible. Draw husks back over kernels, and tie husks with kitchen twine. Soak corn in cold water to cover for 10 minutes.

3. Grill corn, uncovered if using a charcoal grill, for a total of 8–10 minutes, turning it with tongs every 1½–2 minutes. Corn is done when husks are charred and outline of kernels is visible.

4. Remove corn from the grill, and when cool enough to handle, remove and discard husks and any remaining corn silks. To serve, brush corn with melted butter, and season with salt and pepper to taste. Serve immediately.

Grilled Corn

Rosemary Potatoes

Yield: 4–6 servings | Active time: 20 minutes | Start to finish: 1 hour

1. Soak bamboo skewers in warm water to cover, and prepare a medium-hot grill according to the instructions given in Chapter 1.

2. Place potatoes in a saucepan, and cover with cold water. Salt water, and bring potatoes to a boil over high heat. Reduce the heat to medium-high, and boil potatoes for 10–12 minutes, or until just tender. Drain potatoes, and toss them with ¼ cup olive oil, rosemary, salt, and pepper.

3. Thread potatoes onto two parallel skewers. Grill potatoes, uncovered if using a charcoal grill, for a total of 4–5 minutes, turning them with tongs occasionally, or until grill marks appear. Remove skewers from the grill, and drizzle with remaining olive oil. Serve immediately.

VARIATION: *In place of rosemary, try fresh oregano or basil in this recipe, and you can add a few crushed garlic cloves to the oil too.*

8–12 (8-inch) bamboo skewers

1½ pounds baby potatoes, no more than 2 inches in diameter, scrubbed and halved

Salt to taste

⅓ cup olive oil, divided

3 tablespoons finely chopped fresh rosemary

Freshly ground black pepper to taste

Herbed Zucchini

Yield: 4–6 servings | Active time: 15 minutes | Start to finish: 35 minutes

1. Prepare a medium-hot grill according to the instructions given in Chapter 1.

2. Cut zucchini in half lengthwise. Cut a thin slice off the curved side of each half with a paring knife so that zucchini sit securely on the counter. Combine oil, oregano, parsley, thyme, garlic, salt, and pepper in a blender. Puree until smooth, and scrape mixture into a small bowl.

3. Brush both sides of zucchini halves with oil mixture, and grill for 4–5 minutes per side, uncovered if using a charcoal grill, turning slices with tongs. Serve immediately or at room temperature.

Note: Both the zucchini and the oil mixture can be prepared up to 6 hours in advance and refrigerated separately, tightly covered.

4–6 small zucchini, rinsed and trimmed

⅓ cup extra-virgin olive oil

2 tablespoons chopped fresh oregano or 2 teaspoons dried

¼ cup firmly packed fresh parsley leaves

2 teaspoons chopped fresh thyme or ½ teaspoon dried

1 garlic clove, peeled

Salt and freshly ground black pepper to taste

4 medium ripe tomatoes

2 tablespoons extra-virgin olive oil

1 garlic clove, peeled and pressed through a garlic press

1 teaspoon dried oregano

1 teaspoon dried thyme

Salt and freshly ground black pepper

⅔ cup Greek Feta Sauce (recipe on page 22)

Herbed Tomatoes with Greek Feta Sauce

Yield: 4 servings | Active time: 10 minutes | Start to finish: 35 minutes

1. Prepare a medium-hot grill according to the instructions given in Chapter 1. Cut tomatoes in half, and squeeze gently to remove seeds.

2. Combine oil, garlic, oregano, thyme, salt, and pepper in a small bowl, and stir well. Brush mixture on both sides of tomato halves.

3. Grill tomatoes skin-side up, uncovered if using a charcoal grill, for 3–4 minutes, or until grill marks show. Turn tomatoes gently with tongs and grill for an additional 2–3 minutes, or until hot. Serve immediately, passing Greek Feta Sauce separately.

Herbed Tomatoes with Greek Feta Sauce

Sesame Radicchio

Yield: 4–6 servings | Active time: 20 minutes | Start to finish: 45 minutes

1. Prepare a medium-hot grill according to the instructions given in Chapter 1.

2. Trim root end from radicchio, and cut each head into quarters, leaving core attached. Brush radicchio and scallions with 2 tablespoons sesame oil, and sprinkle with salt and pepper. Set aside.

3. Combine vinegar, soy sauce, wine, garlic, ginger, and pepper in a jar with a tight-fitting lid, and shake well. Add remaining sesame oil and vegetable oil, and shake well again. Set aside.

4. Grill radicchio for 3 minutes per side, covered, turning wedges with tongs. Grill scallions for a total of 4 minutes, turning them once. Remove vegetables from the grill.

5. Cut core from radicchio wedges, and cut each wedge crosswise into ½-inch strips. Cut scallions into thirds. Transfer vegetables to a mixing bowl, and toss with dressing. Sprinkle with sesame seeds, and serve immediately.

Note: The dressing can be prepared up to 1 day in advance and refrigerated, tightly covered. Allow it to reach room temperature before using.

3 (4-inch) heads radicchio

12 scallions, white parts and 1 inch of green tops, rinsed and trimmed

¼ cup Asian sesame oil,* divided

Salt and freshly ground black pepper to taste

¼ cup rice wine vinegar

2 tablespoons soy sauce

1 tablespoon mirin* or sherry

2 garlic cloves, peeled and minced

2 teaspoons grated fresh ginger

¼ cup vegetable oil

3 tablespoons sesame seeds, toasted

* Available in the Asian aisle of most supermarkets and in specialty markets.

Mixed Vegetable Kebabs

Yield: 4–6 servings | Active time: 20 minutes | Start to finish: 45 minutes

1. Soak bamboo skewers in warm water to cover, and prepare a medium-hot grill according to the instructions given in Chapter 1.

2. Mix garlic with oil, and set aside. Cut onion in half horizontally, and then cut halves into 8 wedges each. Cut bell peppers into 1½-inch squares. Cut eggplant into 1½-inch cubes. Cut zucchini into 1½-inch segments. Cut mushroom caps into eighths.

3. Rub all vegetables with garlic oil, and sprinkle with salt and pepper.

4. Thread vegetables alternately onto two parallel skewers. Grill kebabs, covered, giving them quarter turns every 2½–3 minutes, for a total of 10–12 minutes, or until vegetables are tender. Remove kebabs from the grill, and serve immediately.

Note: The kebabs can be prepared for grilling up to 6 hours in advance and kept at room temperature.

8–12 (8-inch) bamboo skewers

3 garlic cloves, peeled and minced

¼ cup olive oil

1 red onion, peeled

2 orange or yellow bell peppers, seeds and ribs removed, and halved

1 Italian eggplant

2 small zucchini, trimmed

2 portobello mushroom caps, wiped with a damp paper towel

Salt and freshly ground black pepper to taste

Chapter 15

Non-Grilled Side Dishes

While there are recipes for vegetable and other side dishes in this book that are cooked on the grill, there are many times that the grill is reserved for the entree, and the supporting players are created in the kitchen. It is in this chapter that you will find those recipes.

Condiments like salsa and guacamole are commonly served with all Tex-Mex and other Southwestern dishes, as are variations on beans. Corn in all forms also remains important in the region, and in addition to the recipes in this chapter, there are a few for Grilled Corn in Chapter 14.

---

5 large ripe tomatoes, cored, seeded, and chopped

½ red onion, peeled and finely chopped

½ red bell pepper, seeds and ribs removed, and finely chopped

1 or 2 small jalapeño or serrano chiles, seeds and ribs removed, and finely chopped

4 garlic cloves, peeled and minced

3 tablespoons chopped fresh cilantro

1 tablespoon chopped fresh oregano or 1 teaspoon dried

1 tablespoon chopped fresh basil or ½ teaspoon dried

¼ cup red wine vinegar

2 tablespoons olive oil

Salt and freshly ground black pepper to taste

Summer Tomato Salsa

Yield: 4 cups | Active time: 15 minutes | Start to finish: 1¼ hours, including 1 hour for chilling

1. Combine tomatoes, onion, red pepper, chiles, garlic, cilantro, oregano, basil, vinegar, and olive oil in a glass or stainless-steel bowl.

2. Stir gently, and refrigerate for at least 1 hour to blend the flavors. Season to taste with salt and pepper. Serve immediately.

Note: The salsa can be prepared up to 1 day in advance and refrigerated, tightly covered.

Summer Tomato Salsa

Guacamole

Guacamole

Yield: 3 cups | Active time: 15 minutes | Start to finish: 15 minutes

1. Place avocados in a bowl with red onion and chiles and, using a table fork, mash mixture together, leaving some avocado in small chunks.

2. Stir in cilantro and lime juice, and season to taste with salt and pepper. Serve immediately.

Note: The guacamole can be made up to 8 hours in advance; push a sheet of plastic wrap directly into the surface to prevent discoloration, and then refrigerate until ready to serve.

5 ripe avocados, peeled, seeded, and diced

1 small red onion, peeled and finely diced

1 or 2 jalapeño or serrano chiles, seeds and ribs removed, and finely chopped

½ cup chopped fresh cilantro

2 tablespoons freshly squeezed lime juice, or to taste

Salt and freshly ground black pepper to taste

4 large ripe tomatoes, cored, seeded, and chopped

½ medium red onion, peeled and chopped

3 garlic cloves, peeled and minced

¼ cup chopped fresh cilantro

1 jalapeño or serrano chile, seeds and ribs removed, and finely chopped

3 tablespoons freshly squeezed lime juice

3 tablespoons olive oil

Salt and freshly ground black pepper to taste

Pico de Gallo

Yield: 2 cups | Active time: 15 minutes | Start to finish: 30 minutes

Combine tomatoes, onion, garlic, cilantro, chile, lime juice, olive oil, salt, and pepper in a mixing bowl, and stir well. Allow mixture to sit at room temperature for 15 minutes so that flavors will blend.

Note: The relish can be prepared up to 6 hours in advance and kept at room temperature; drain off excess liquid before serving.

---

1 pound dried pinto beans

2 bay leaves

1 tablespoon dried oregano

¼ pound bacon, cut into 1-inch segments

1 large onion, peeled and diced

1 large green bell pepper, seeds and ribs removed, and diced

3 garlic cloves, peeled and minced

2 tablespoons cider vinegar

Salt and freshly ground black pepper to taste

Stewed Beans

Yield: 6–8 servings | Active time: 20 minutes | Start to finish: 3 hours, including 1 hour for soaking

1. Place beans in a 4-quart saucepan and cover with cold water. Bring to a boil over high heat, covered, and boil for 1 minute. Remove the pan from the heat, and allow beans to soak for 1 hour, covered. (Alternatively, soak beans in water to cover for a minimum of 6 hours or preferably overnight. With either method, cooking should progress as soon as the beans are soaked.) Drain beans, and return to the saucepan.

2. Cover beans with fresh water, add bay leaves and oregano, and bring to a boil over medium-high heat, stirring occasionally. Reduce the heat to low and simmer beans, covered, for 1 hour, or until beans are almost tender. Drain beans, reserving 2 cups of liquid. Remove and discard bay leaves. Return beans and reserved liquid to the saucepan.

3. While beans simmer, place bacon in a large skillet over medium-high heat. Cook until bacon is crisp, then remove bacon from the pan with a slotted spoon, and drain on paper towels. Discard all but 3 tablespoons of bacon fat.

4. Add onion, bell pepper, and garlic to the skillet and cook over medium-high heat, stirring frequently, for 3 minutes, or until onion is translucent.

5. Add vegetables, vinegar, and bacon to beans, and stir well. Bring beans back to a boil, and simmer, uncovered, for 30 minutes or until very tender. Season to taste with salt and pepper, and serve hot.

Note: The beans can be prepared up to 2 days in advance and refrigerated, tightly covered. Reheat the beans over low heat, covered.

Refried Black Beans

Yield: 8–10 servings | Active time: 25 minutes | Start to finish: 2 hours

1. Rinse beans in a colander, picking over them well to remove any pebbles or broken beans. Place beans in a stockpot with water to cover by 3 inches, and bring to a boil over high heat. Reduce the heat to low, and simmer beans, partially covered, for 1 hour.

2. Add ½ of onion, garlic, and chicken stock, and simmer for an additional 30 minutes, or until beans are very tender.

3. While beans simmer, cook bacon in a deep skillet over medium-high heat until very crisp. Remove bacon from the pan with a slotted spoon, and discard all but 4 tablespoons of bacon fat. Add remaining onion, chiles, and scallions to the pan, and cook over medium-high heat for 3 minutes, or until onions are translucent, stirring frequently.

4. Drain cooked beans, reserving bean broth. Place beans, bacon, and vegetable mixture in a blender or food processor along with 3 cups of bean broth; this will have to be done in batches. Process until mixture is pureed but the consistency is still chunky. Stir in a mixing bowl to combine various batches of puree.

5. Heat oil in a deep, heavy skillet over medium heat, and add beans. Cook over low heat, stirring constantly, until beans are thick and some of liquid has evaporated, about 10 minutes. Season to taste with salt and pepper, and stir in cilantro. Serve immediately, sprinkled with grated cheese.

Note: The starch in the beans will thicken the mixture when it cools. The beans can be cooked and pureed up to 6 hours in advance; however, do not refry them until just prior to serving.

1 pound dried black beans

1 medium onion, peeled and chopped, divided

2 garlic cloves, peeled and minced

2 cups chicken stock

½ pound bacon, sliced into ½-inch pieces

3 jalapeño or serrano chiles, seeds and ribs removed, and chopped

3 scallions, white parts and 3 inches of green tops, rinsed, trimmed, and chopped

3 tablespoons vegetable oil

Salt and freshly ground black pepper to taste

¼ cup chopped fresh cilantro

1½ cups grated Monterey Jack cheese

Southwestern Pinto Bean Salad

Yield: 6–8 servings | Active time: 15 minutes | Start to finish: 45 minutes, including 30 minutes for chilling

1. Combine beans, tomatoes, corn, cilantro, and onion in a mixing bowl.

2. Combine mayonnaise, garlic, chipotle chile, and cumin in a blender or in a food processor fitted with a steel blade. Puree until smooth. Season to taste with salt and pepper, and stir dressing into salad. Refrigerate for at least 30 minutes or until cold, and serve.

Note: The salad can be made up to 1 day in advance and refrigerated, tightly covered.

2 (15-ounce) cans pinto beans, drained and rinsed

3 ripe plum tomatoes, rinsed, cored, seeded, and cut into ½-inch dice

1 cup cooked corn kernels

¼ cup chopped fresh cilantro

¼ small red onion, peeled and diced

⅓ cup mayonnaise

2 garlic cloves, peeled

1 chipotle chile in adobo sauce, drained

2 teaspoons ground cumin

Salt and freshly ground black pepper to taste

1 cup yellow cornmeal

1 cup all-purpose flour

1½ teaspoons baking powder

½ teaspoon baking soda

¼ teaspoon salt

2 large eggs

¾ cup buttermilk

½ cup canned creamed corn

5 tablespoons unsalted butter, melted

Cornbread

Yield: 6–8 servings | Active time: 10 minutes | Start to finish: 30 minutes

1. Preheat the oven to 425˚F, and grease a 9-inch-square pan generously.

2. Whisk together cornmeal, flour, baking powder, baking soda, and salt in a large mixing bowl. Whisk together eggs, buttermilk, creamed corn, and butter in a small bowl. Add buttermilk mixture to cornmeal mixture, and stir batter until just blended.

3. Heat the greased pan in the oven for 3 minutes, or until it is very hot. Remove the pan from the oven, and spread batter in it evenly. Bake cornbread in the middle of the oven for 15 minutes, or until top is pale golden and the sides begin to pull away from the edges of the pan.

4. Allow cornbread to cool for 5 minutes, then turn it out onto a rack. Cut into pieces, and serve hot or at room temperature.

VARIATION: *Use some chopped pimiento in the cornbread, and for a sweeter bread feel free to add 2 tablespoons of granulated sugar.*

Note: The cornbread is best eaten within a few hours of baking.

Cornbread

Corn Fritters

Yield: 8–10 servings | Active time: 25 minutes | Start to finish: 25 minutes

1. Place corn in a saucepan, and cover with salted water. Bring to a boil over high heat, and cook for 2 minutes. Drain, and place corn in a blender or in a food processor fitted with a steel blade. Add eggs, and puree until smooth. Scrape mixture into a mixing bowl.

2. Stir onions, scallions, garlic, and cilantro into corn. Combine flour, cornmeal, sugar, baking powder, coriander, salt, and pepper in another mixing bowl, and whisk well. Stir dry ingredients into corn mixture, stirring until just combined.

3. Heat oil in a deep-sided saucepan or deep-fryer to a temperature of 375°F. Preheat the oven to 150°F, and line a baking sheet with paper towels.

4. Using a rubber spatula, push batter carefully into hot fat, about 1 tablespoonful at a time. Fry fritters until they are a deep golden brown, turning them in the hot fat to brown both sides. Remove fritters from the pan with a slotted spoon, and drain on paper towels. Keep fritters warm in the oven while frying remaining batter. Serve immediately.

Note: The fritters can be prepared up to 2 days in advance and refrigerated, tightly covered. Reheat in a 375°F oven for 5–7 minutes, or until hot and crispy.

- 2 pounds whole corn kernels (either cut fresh from the cob or frozen and thawed; do not use canned corn)
- 3 large eggs
- 2 medium onions, peeled and chopped
- 2 scallions, white parts only, rinsed, trimmed, and chopped
- 1 garlic clove, peeled and minced
- 3 tablespoons chopped fresh cilantro
- 1¼ cups all-purpose flour
- ½ cup yellow cornmeal
- 1 tablespoon granulated sugar
- 1½ tablespoons baking powder
- 1½ tablespoons ground coriander
- Salt and freshly ground black pepper to taste
- 3–4 cups vegetable oil

Jicama Slaw

Yield: 4–6 servings | Active time: 20 minutes | Start to finish: 35 minutes

1. Combine jicama, red pepper, orange pepper, and onion in a mixing bowl. Combine lime juice, cilantro, oil, salt, and pepper in a jar with a tight-fitting lid, and shake well.

2. Pour dressing over vegetables, and toss to combine. Allow slaw to sit for at least 15 minutes for flavors to blend.

Note: The slaw can be made up to 1 day in advance and refrigerated, tightly covered. Allow it to reach room temperature before serving.

- 1 medium jicama, peeled and cut into matchstick strips
- 1 red bell pepper, seeds and ribs removed, and cut into matchstick strips
- 1 orange bell pepper, seeds and ribs removed, and cut into matchstick strips
- ½ small red onion, peeled and cut into matchstick strips
- 3 tablespoons freshly squeezed lime juice
- 3 tablespoons chopped fresh cilantro
- 2 tablespoons olive oil
- Salt and freshly ground black pepper to taste

½ cup granulated sugar

½ cup cider vinegar

⅓ cup vegetable oil

1 tablespoon celery seeds

1 tablespoon dry mustard

Salt and freshly ground black pepper to taste

1 (2-pound) head green cabbage, cored and shredded

1 small red onion, peeled and thinly sliced

1 green bell pepper, seeds and ribs removed, and thinly sliced

1 red bell pepper, seeds and ribs removed, and thinly sliced

Celery Seed Slaw

Yield: 6–8 servings | Active time: 20 minutes | Start to finish: 5½ hours, including 5 hours to marinate and chill

1. Combine sugar, vinegar, and oil in a small saucepan, and bring to a boil over medium heat, stirring occasionally. Reduce the heat to low and stir in celery seed, mustard, salt, and pepper. Simmer for 2 minutes, stirring occasionally.

2. Combine cabbage, onion, green pepper, and red pepper in a large mixing bowl. Toss dressing with salad. Allow slaw to sit at room temperature for 2 hours, tossing it occasionally. Refrigerate slaw for 3–4 hours. Drain well before serving.

Note: The slaw can be made 1 day in advance and refrigerated, tightly covered with plastic wrap.

2 pounds small redskin potatoes, scrubbed

salt to taste

1 cucumber, peeled

1 green bell pepper, seeds and ribs removed

1 small red onion, peeled

3 celery ribs, trimmed

½ cup mayonnaise

3 tablespoons white wine vinegar

Freshly ground black pepper to taste

Garden Potato Salad

Yield: 6–8 servings | Active time: 20 minutes | Start to finish: 4 hours, including 3 hours to chill

1. Place potatoes in a large saucepan of cold salted water. Bring potatoes to a boil over high heat, reduce the heat to medium, and boil potatoes for 10–20 minutes, or until they are tender when pierced with the tip of a paring knife. Drain potatoes and chill well. Cut potatoes into 1-inch cubes, and place them in a large mixing bowl.

2. Cut cucumber in half lengthwise and scrape out the seeds with a teaspoon. Slice cucumber into thin arcs, and add to potatoes. Cut green pepper into 1-inch sections and slice each section into thin strips. Add to the mixing bowl. Cut onion in half through the root end, and cut each half into thirds. Cut into thin slices and add to the mixing bowl. Cut each celery rib in half lengthwise and thinly slice the celery. Add to the mixing bowl.

3. Toss potato salad with mayonnaise and vinegar, and season to taste with salt and pepper. Serve well chilled.

Note: The salad can be made 1 day in advance and refrigerated, tightly covered.

Chapter 16

Grilled Desserts

The title of this chapter is not an oxymoron, nor is it just variations on toasted marshmallows—although there is a recipe for S'mores leading it off. What you will find when cooking these recipes is that the grill is a natural way to glean the most luscious flavor from fruit; fruit desserts comprise the majority of these recipes. It should come as no surprise that heating enhances the fruits' natural sweetness, as well as creating a softer texture.

Ultimately Messy S'mores

Yield: 4–6 servings | Active time: 10 minutes | Start to finish: 35 minutes

1. Prepare a medium-hot grill according to the instructions given in Chapter 1. Cut 12 (8-inch) squares of aluminum foil.

2. Place 1 cracker in the center of each foil sheet, and top with chocolate. Toast marshmallows over the grill on a long-handled fork, and place on top of chocolate. Top marshmallows with remaining crackers, and enclose sandwiches in foil.

3. Grill foil packets for 2 minutes, or until chocolate is melted and gooey. Unwrap, and serve immediately.

24 sweet whole-wheat crackers, such as Carr's wheatmeal biscuits, or graham crackers

1½ (3-ounce) dark chocolate bars or any flavored chocolate bar, broken into ½-inch pieces

12 large marshmallows

Ultimately Messy S'mores

8 (8-inch) flour tortillas

Vegetable oil spray

1 (8-ounce) package cream cheese, softened

4 (2-ounce) candy bars, such as Snickers, Almond Joy, Milky Way, or any chocolate bar, each cut into 15 thin slices

4 tablespoons confectioners' sugar

Candy Bar Quesadillas

Yield: 4–6 servings | Active time: 10 minutes | Start to finish: 30 minutes

1. Prepare a medium-hot grill according to the instructions given in Chapter 1.

2. Wrap tortillas in plastic wrap and microwave on high (100% power) for 20 seconds, or until pliable. Spray 4 tortillas with vegetable oil spray, and place them sprayed-side down on a cookie sheet. Spread each tortilla with one-quarter of cream cheese to within ½ inch of the edge. Top cheese with candy bar slices.

3. Top with remaining 4 tortillas, and press with the palm of your hand or a spatula to close them firmly. Spray tops of quesadillas with vegetable oil spray.

4. Grill quesadillas, covered, for 2 minutes. Turn gently with a wide spatula and grill for an additional 2 minutes, or until brown and crisp. Remove quesadillas from the grill, and sprinkle with confectioners' sugar. Allow quesadillas to sit for 2 minutes, then cut each into 6 sections and serve immediately.

Note: The quesadillas can be prepared 1 day in advance of grilling them. Refrigerate them, tightly covered with plastic wrap, and bring them back to room temperature before grilling.

1 pint fresh strawberries, rinsed, stemmed, and sliced, divided

½ pint fresh raspberries, rinsed

½ pint fresh blueberries, rinsed

2 tablespoons crème de cassis or Chambord

1 teaspoon grated lemon zest

4–6 (¾-inch) slices pound cake, homemade or purchased

1 pint strawberry ice cream, or your favorite flavor

Toasted Cake with Berry Sauce

Yield: 4–6 servings | Active time: 15 minutes | Start to finish: 30 minutes

1. Prepare a medium-hot grill according to the instructions given in Chapter 1.

2. Place half of strawberries in a food processor fitted with a steel blade or in a blender; puree until smooth. Combine puree, remaining strawberries, raspberries, blueberries, crème de cassis, and lemon zest in a mixing bowl, and stir well. Refrigerate, tightly covered, until ready to use.

3. Grill cake slices, uncovered if using a charcoal grill, for 1 minute per side or until grill marks appear. To serve, place cake slices on plates and top with ice cream and fruit sauce. Serve immediately.

Note: Fruit sauce can be made up to 1 day in advance and chilled, tightly covered.

Pineapple with Dulce de Leche

Yield: 6–8 servings | Active time: 15 minutes | Start to finish: 3½ hours

2 (14-ounce) cans sweetened condensed milk

¼ cup dark rum

1 teaspoon pure vanilla extract, preferably Mexican

1 ripe pineapple

3–4 cups vanilla ice cream

1. Remove the labels from the cans, stand the cans in a deep stockpot, and fill the pot with hot water. Cover the pan, and bring to a boil over high heat, then reduce the heat to low and allow the cans to simmer gently for 3 hours. Add water as necessary to keep the cans covered. Remove the cans from the water with tongs and allow them to cool. Pour contents of the cans into a mixing bowl, and whisk in rum and vanilla. Keep warm.

2. Prepare a medium-hot grill according to the instructions given in Chapter 1.

3. While cans simmer, cut rind off pineapple, and cut in half vertically. Cut out and discard core, and cut pineapple into ⅓-inch slices. Set aside.

4. Grill pineapple slices for 1½–2 minutes per side, uncovered if using a charcoal grill, or until browned. To serve, place pineapple slices on plates and top with ice cream and sauce. Serve immediately.

Note: The sauce can be made up to 2 days in advance and refrigerated, tightly covered. Reheat it over low heat or in a microwave oven before using.

Grilled Banana Splits

Yield: 4–6 servings | Active time: 10 minutes | Start to finish: 30 minutes

4–6 ripe bananas, unpeeled

2 tablespoons firmly packed light brown sugar

1 teaspoon ground cinnamon

8–12 small scoops vanilla ice cream

1 cup Chocolate Sauce (recipe follows), heated

½ cup coarsely chopped toasted walnuts

Sweetened whipped cream (optional)

4–6 maraschino cherries or strawberries (optional)

1. Prepare a medium-hot grill according to the instructions given in Chapter 1.

2. Slice unpeeled bananas in half lengthwise and crosswise so each banana is cut into quarters. Mix sugar and cinnamon, and rub mixture into cut sides of bananas.

3. Grill bananas cut-side down for 2 minutes, or until grill marks appear. Turn bananas and grill an additional 2–3 minutes, or until bananas are soft.

4. To serve, remove skin from bananas, and place 4 pieces in the bottom of each serving bowl. Top bananas with 2 scoops ice cream, chocolate sauce, and 1–2 tablespoons chopped nuts. Top with whipped cream and cherries, if using. Serve immediately.

5 ounces good-quality
  bittersweet chocolate

½ cup heavy cream

3 tablespoons
  unsweetened cocoa
  powder

1 tablespoon rum

¼ teaspoon pure vanilla
  extract

Pinch of salt

Chocolate Sauce

Yield: 1½ cups | Active time: 10 minutes | Start to finish: 15 minutes

1. Chop chocolate into pieces no larger than a lima bean, and set aside.

2. Pour cream into a 1-quart saucepan, and place over medium heat. Whisk in cocoa powder, rum, vanilla, and salt. Bring to a boil, whisking frequently, until mixture is smooth.

3. When cream begins to boil, remove pan from the heat. Add chocolate, cover pan, and allow to sit for 5 minutes; whisk well until sauce is smooth. If lumps remain, place sauce over low heat and continue to whisk until smooth.

4. Scrape mixture into a container, and refrigerate for up to 1 week or freeze for up to 3 months. To serve, microwave sauce on medium (50% power) for 30-second intervals or until liquid and warm, stirring well between microwave times.

4–6 navel oranges

1 pint fresh raspberries,
  rinsed

2 tablespoons granulated
  sugar

2 tablespoons Grand
  Marnier, triple sec, or
  another orange-flavored
  liqueur

1 pint vanilla ice cream or
  vanilla frozen yogurt

Grilled Oranges with Raspberry Sauce

Yield: 4–6 servings | Active time: 10 minutes | Start to finish: 30 minutes

1. Prepare a medium-hot grill according to the instructions given in Chapter 1.

2. Grate 2 teaspoons zest off oranges, and then peel oranges. Cut each into 4 slices horizontally. Combine raspberries, sugar, Grand Marnier, and orange zest in a small mixing bowl. Mash raspberries gently, and set aside.

3. Grill orange slices for 1½–2 minutes per side, uncovered if using a charcoal grill, or until browned. To serve, arrange orange slices on the bottom of bowls, and top with ice cream and raspberry sauce. Serve immediately.

Note: The raspberry sauce can be made up to 6 hours in advance and kept at room temperature.

Nouvelle Peach Melba

Yield: 4–6 servings | Active time: 20 minutes | Start to finish: 30 minutes

1. Prepare a medium-hot grill according to the instructions given in Chapter 1.

2. Cut peaches in half and discard stones. Place peaches in a 9 x 13-inch pan, cut-side up.

3. Combine ⅔ cup sugar, orange juice, 1 tablespoon lemon juice, and vanilla in a small saucepan, and stir well. Bring to a boil over medium-high heat, and boil for 2 minutes, stirring occasionally. Pour syrup over peaches, and set aside.

4. Combine raspberries, remaining sugar, remaining lemon juice, and Chambord in a food processor fitted with a steel blade or in a blender. Puree until smooth, and strain mixture. Refrigerate until ready to use.

5. Drain peaches, and grill skin-side up for 4 minutes, uncovered if using a charcoal grill, then turn peaches with tongs and grill skin-side down for an additional 3–4 minutes, or until peaches are tender. To serve, place 2 peach halves in the bottom of each bowl, and top with ice cream and raspberry sauce. Serve immediately.

Note: Raspberry sauce can be made up to 1 day in advance and refrigerated, tightly covered.

4–6 ripe peaches, unpeeled

¾ cup granulated sugar, divided

⅔ cup freshly squeezed orange juice

2 tablespoons freshly squeezed lemon juice, divided

¼ teaspoon pure vanilla extract

1 pint fresh raspberries, rinsed, or 1 (8-ounce) package frozen dry-packed raspberries, thawed

2 tablespoons Chambord or other berry-flavored liqueur

1 pint vanilla ice cream

Nouvelle Peach Melba

Chapter 17

Other Sweet Endings

Creamy custards as well as fruit desserts and chocolate are all hallmarks of desserts in the Southwestern states; in this chapter you will find them all represented. But desserts such as Strawberry Shortcake are national favorites, and my version of that tried-and-true American invention is here too.

¾ cup granulated sugar

3 large eggs

3 large egg yolks

2 teaspoons pure vanilla extract

1 (14-ounce) can sweetened condensed milk

1¾ cups whole milk

1 (3-ounce) package cream cheese, softened

Flan

Yield: 6 servings | Active time: 15 minutes | Start to finish: 3 hours, including 1½ hours for cooling

1. Place sugar in a small skillet over medium-high heat, and stir while sugar melts. Allow sugar to boil and turn a walnut brown, stirring occasionally. Watch caramel carefully so that it does not burn.

2. Pour caramel into the bottom of a 9-inch flan pan or soufflé dish and, working quickly, spread it evenly with a rubber spatula over the bottom of the pan.

3. Preheat the oven to 350°F. Combine eggs, egg yolks, vanilla, sweetened condensed milk, whole milk, and cream cheese in a blender or a food processor fitted with a steel blade. Process for 1 minute.

4. Pour mixture into the prepared pan and place the pan in a larger baking pan in the center of the oven. Pour boiling water halfway up the sides of the pan and bake for 1 hour and 10 minutes, or until a knife inserted in the center comes out clean. Cover flan with foil if the top seems to be getting too brown.

5. Remove flan from the oven, allow to cool to room temperature, then cut around the edges and invert onto a deep-sided serving plate. Serve each piece with some caramel syrup that has formed on the bottom of the pan.

Note: The flan can be prepared up to 2 days in advance and refrigerated, tightly covered. Leave it in the pan until ready to serve, and allow it to reach room temperature before serving.

Flan

2 or 3 (1¼ pounds total weight) sweet potatoes or red yams

1½ cups granulated sugar

8 large eggs

2 large egg yolks

1 (14-ounce) can sweetened condensed milk

1 cup heavy cream

1 cup half-and-half

1 teaspoon pure vanilla extract

½ teaspoon ground cinnamon

¼ teaspoon ground allspice

¼ teaspoon ground nutmeg

Pinch of salt

Sweet Potato Flan

Yield: 6–8 servings | Active time: 20 minutes | Start to finish: 4 hours, including 1½ hours for cooling

1. Preheat the oven to 400°F, and line a baking sheet with aluminum foil. Scrub sweet potatoes, and prick with a meat fork. Bake for 1–1½ hours, depending on size, or until soft. Remove sweet potatoes from the oven, peel, cut into chunks, and puree in a blender or a food processor fitted with a steel blade. You should have 1½ cups of puree. Set aside to cool.

2. While sweet potatoes bake, place sugar in a small skillet over medium-high heat and stir while sugar melts. Allow sugar to boil and turn a walnut brown, stirring occasionally. Watch caramel carefully so that it does not burn. Pour caramel into the bottom of a 9-inch flan pan or soufflé dish and, working quickly, spread it evenly with a rubber spatula over the bottom of the pan.

3. Beat eggs and egg yolks in a bowl until light and fluffy. Add sweetened condensed milk, cream, half-and-half, vanilla, cinnamon, allspice, nutmeg, salt, and cooled sweet potato puree, and beat well.

4. Pour mixture into the prepared pan and place the pan in a larger baking pan in the center of the oven. Pour boiling water halfway up the sides of the pan and bake for 1 hour, or until a knife inserted in the center comes out clean. Cover the flan with foil if the top seems to be getting too brown.

5. Remove flan from the oven, allow to cool to room temperature, then cut around the edges and invert onto a deep-sided serving plate. Serve each piece with some of the caramel syrup.

Note: The flan can be prepared up to 2 days in advance and refrigerated, tightly covered. Leave it in the pan until ready to serve.

2 cups all-purpose flour

½ teaspoon baking powder

Salt to taste

½ teaspoon granulated sugar

1½ teaspoons vegetable oil

1 tablespoon evaporated milk

2 tablespoons warm water

Vegetable oil for deep-frying

Honey for serving

Sopaipillas

Yield: 4 dozen | Active time: 25 minutes | Start to finish: 55 minutes, including 30 minutes for dough to rest

1. Place flour in a large mixing bowl and add baking powder, salt, and sugar. Stir well, then add oil, evaporated milk, and water. Using your hands, work the mixture into a dough and knead gently on a floured surface. It will remain slightly sticky.

2. Allow dough to rest for 30 minutes, then divide it into 12 balls by tearing off pieces into nuggets that form balls in your hand.

3. On a floured surface, roll each ball into a 10-inch circle ¼ inch thick.

4. Preheat the oven to 150°F and line a baking sheet with paper towels. Heat 3 inches of oil in a saucepan or deep-fryer to a temperature of 400°F.

5. Cut each circle into quarters and add 4 pieces at a time to hot oil. Using a spatula or spoon, fan hot oil over the top of each triangle, which will cause it to start puffing up. After 20 seconds, turn sopaipillas over and quickly brown the other side. Remove sopaipillas from the pan with a slotted spoon and drain on paper towels. Transfer to the prepared baking sheet, and keep warm while frying remaining dough. Serve immediately with honey.

Note: While you can make the dough up to 6 hours in advance, sopaipillas must be fried at the last minute, and should be made in small batches so they can be eaten hot.

Rice Pudding with Mixed Berries

Yield: 6–8 servings | Active time: 20 minutes | Start to finish: 3 hours, including 2 hours for cooling

3 cups water

1 cup long-grain or medium-grain white rice

½ teaspoon salt

⅓ cup plus 3 tablespoons granulated sugar

½ teaspoon ground cinnamon

2 cups whole milk

1 teaspoon pure vanilla extract

1 pint fresh strawberries, rinsed, hulled, and sliced

1 (6-ounce) package fresh raspberries, rinsed

1 (6-ounce) package fresh blueberries or blackberries, rinsed

2 (4-ounce) containers refrigerated vanilla pudding

1. Bring water to boil in medium saucepan over high heat. Add rice and salt, reduce the heat to medium-low, and simmer rice, uncovered, for 20 minutes, or until rice is very tender and water is absorbed. Add ⅓ cup sugar and cinnamon, and stir to blend. Add milk, and simmer for 25 minutes, stirring frequently, over low heat, or until mixture is very thick. Remove the pan from the heat, and stir in vanilla. Cool to room temperature, about 2 hours.

2. Mix strawberries, raspberries, and blueberries with remaining 3 tablespoons sugar in a large bowl. Let stand for at least 30 minutes or until juices form.

3. Stir vanilla pudding and 2 cups fruit mixture into rice pudding. Transfer to large bowl. Top with remaining fruit, and serve immediately.

VARIATION: *This is a recipe that is open to many variations. The fruit can be chopped peaches, nectarines, or apricots as well as any combination of berries. To trim fat, 2 percent milk can be used, as can nonfat vanilla yogurt in place of the creamier pudding.*

Note: The rice pudding and berry mixture can be prepared 4 hours in advance. Cover and refrigerate separately. Bring to room temperature before continuing.

Strawberry Shortcake

½ pound (2 sticks) unsalted butter, divided

3 cups all-purpose flour

⅓ cup granulated sugar

1 tablespoon cream of tartar

2¼ teaspoons baking soda

¼ teaspoon salt

2 cups heavy cream, divided

1 quart strawberries

⅓ cup crème de cassis or Chambord

⅓ cup confectioners' sugar

Strawberry Shortcake

Yield: 6 servings | Active time: 15 minutes | Start to finish: 40 minutes, including 10 minutes for cooling

1. Preheat the oven to 375°F and grease two baking sheets with 1 tablespoon butter. Combine flour, sugar, cream of tartar, baking soda, and salt in a medium mixing bowl. Melt 3 tablespoons butter, and set aside. Cut remaining butter into ¼-inch cubes.

2. Cut cubed butter into flour mixture using a pastry blender, two knives, or your fingertips until mixture resembles coarse meal. Add 1 cup cream, and blend until just blended.

3. Scrape dough onto a floured surface, and knead lightly. Roll dough to a thickness of ¾ inch. Cut out 6 (4-inch) rounds and place them on the baking sheet. Brush rounds with melted butter. Cut out 6 (2½-inch) rounds and place them on top of larger rounds. Brush tops with butter.

4. Bake for 15–17 minutes or until shortcakes are golden brown. Cool for at least 10 minutes on a wire rack.

5. While shortcakes bake, rinse strawberries, discard green caps, and slice. Toss strawberries with crème de cassis. Set aside. Just prior to serving, whip remaining 1 cup cream with confectioners' sugar until stiff peaks form.

6. To serve, mound strawberries on larger round, and top with whipped cream and smaller round. Serve immediately.

VARIATION: *Any berry can be substituted for the strawberries, as can peeled peach slices.*

Note: The shortcakes can be baked up to 6 hours in advance and kept at room temperature.

Warm Chocolate Tortes

Yield: 6 servings | Active time: 20 minutes | Start to finish: 35 minutes

6 tablespoons (¾ stick) unsalted butter, divided

5 ounces bittersweet chocolate, chopped, divided

2 tablespoons heavy cream

1 tablespoon rum or fruit-flavored liqueur

2 large eggs

1 large egg yolk

¼ cup granulated sugar

¼ cup all-purpose flour

Sweetened whipped cream or ice cream (optional)

1. Grease six muffin cups with 1 tablespoon butter. Melt 2 ounces chocolate with cream and rum in a small microwave-safe dish. Stir well and refrigerate to harden. Form chocolate into 6 balls and refrigerate until ready to use.

2. Preheat the oven to 350°F. Melt remaining chocolate with remaining butter and allow to cool.

3. Combine eggs, egg yolk, and sugar in a medium mixing bowl. Beat with an electric mixer at medium and then high speed until very thick and triple in volume. Fold cooled chocolate into eggs, and then fold in flour.

4. Divide batter among the muffin cups and push a chocolate ball into the center of each cup. Bake tortes for 10–12 minutes, or until sides are set. Remove the muffin pan from the oven and invert tortes onto a baking sheet. Move tortes to individual serving plates, and serve immediately, with whipped cream or ice cream, if using.

Note: The tortes can be prepared up to 2 hours before baking them.

1 cup creamy peanut butter

¾ cup granulated sugar

1 (8-ounce) package cream cheese, softened

1 tablespoon unsalted butter, melted

1 teaspoon pure vanilla extract

1¾ cups heavy cream, divided

6 ounces bittersweet chocolate

1 (9-inch) chocolate cookie or graham cracker crumb crust

Peanut Butter Mousse Pie

Yield: 6–8 servings | Active time: 25 minutes | Start to finish: 2½ hours, including 2 hours for chilling

1. Beat peanut butter and sugar with an electric mixer on medium speed until light and fluffy. Add cream cheese, butter, and vanilla and beat well. In another mixing bowl, whip ¾ cup cream until medium-soft peaks form, and fold it into peanut butter mixture until thoroughly combined. Refrigerate 30 minutes, or until slightly firm.

2. While mousse chills, chop chocolate into small pieces and place it in a mixing bowl. Bring remaining 1 cup cream to a boil over low heat in a small saucepan and pour it over chocolate. Stir until melted and thoroughly combined. Pour chocolate into pie shell, reserving about ⅓ cup at room temperature. Chill until firmly set.

3. Remove mousse from the refrigerator. Beat with an electric mixer on low speed for at least 5 minutes, preferably longer, until mousse is light and fluffy. Cover chocolate layer with the peanut butter mousse and distribute it evenly with a spatula. Place remaining chocolate in a pastry bag fitted with the small tip or in a plastic bag with small hole at one corner. Drizzle it decoratively over the mousse. Chill until ready to serve.

Note: The pie can be prepared 1 day in advance and refrigerated, loosely covered with plastic wrap.

1 cup granulated sugar, divided

1 tablespoon grated orange zest

1½ teaspoons anise seeds

3 cups all-purpose flour

1 teaspoon baking powder

½ teaspoon salt

1 cup lard

1 teaspoon ground cinnamon

1 large egg, lightly beaten

Biscochitos

Yield: 3 dozen | Active time: 25 minutes | Start to finish: 1 hour, including 20 minutes for cooling

1. Preheat the oven to 350°F, and lightly grease two baking sheets.

2. Combine ⅔ cup sugar and orange zest in a small bowl, and set aside. Place anise seeds in a small dry skillet, and toast for 2 minutes over medium heat, or until fragrant. Set aside.

3. Combine flour, baking powder, salt, and anise seed in a mixing bowl, and whisk well. In another large mixing bowl, beat lard with an electric mixer at medium speed until light and fluffy. Beat in sugar and beat for 2 minutes. Stir in dry ingredients, and mix until dough forms a mass. Roll dough to a thickness of ¼ inch on a floured surface. Cut out cookies in any shape you choose.

4. For topping, combine remaining sugar and cinnamon in a small bowl. Brush cookies with egg, and sprinkle with sugar mixture. Transfer cookies to prepared baking sheets with a spatula. Bake cookies for 8–10 minutes or until lightly browned. Cool cookies completely on a cooling rack.

Note: The cookies can be baked up to 2 days in advance. Once cooled, they can be stored at room temperature in an airtight container.

Mexican Wedding Cookies

Yield: 36 cookies | Active time: 15 minutes | Start to finish: 45 minutes, including 15 minutes for cooling

1. Preheat the oven to 350°F, and lightly grease two baking sheets.

2. Place butter in a mixing bowl with 1¼ cups sugar, and beat well at medium speed with an electric mixer until light and fluffy. Add cake flour, self-rising flour, almonds, and vanilla to the bowl, and mix briefly until just combined. The dough will be very stiff; add a few drops of hot water, if necessary, to make it pliable.

3. Take 1-tablespoon bits of dough, and roll them into balls. Place balls 1 inch apart on the prepared baking sheets, and flatten balls with the bottom of glass dipped in flour. Bake cookies for 12–15 minutes, or until lightly browned. Remove cookies from the oven.

4. Place remaining ½ cup sugar in a low bowl, and transfer cookies a few at a time to the bowl with a spatula. Coat cookies with sugar, and then transfer them to a cooling rack to cool completely.

½ pound (2 sticks) unsalted butter, softened

1¾ cups confectioners' sugar, divided

1 cup cake flour

1 cup self-rising flour

1 cup blanched almonds, very finely chopped

½ teaspoon pure vanilla extract, preferably Mexican

Appendix A

Metric Conversion Tables

The scientifically precise calculations needed for baking are not necessary when cooking conventionally. The tables in this appendix are designed for general cooking. If making conversions for baking, grab your calculator and compute the exact figure.

Converting Ounces to Grams

The numbers in the following table are approximate. To reach the exact number of grams, multiply the number of ounces by 28.35.

OUNCES	GRAMS
1 ounce	30 grams
2 ounces	60 grams
3 ounces	85 grams
4 ounces	115 grams
5 ounces	140 grams
6 ounces	180 grams
7 ounces	200 grams
8 ounces	225 grams
9 ounces	250 grams
10 ounces	285 grams
11 ounces	300 grams
12 ounces	340 grams
13 ounces	370 grams
14 ounces	400 grams
15 ounces	425 grams
16 ounces	450 grams

Converting Quarts to Liters

The numbers in the following table are approximate. To reach the exact number of liters, multiply the number of quarts by 0.95.

QUARTS	LITERS
1 cup (¼ quart)	¼ liter
1 pint (½ quart)	½ liter
1 quart	1 liter
2 quarts	2 liters
2½ quarts	2½ liters
3 quarts	2¾ liters
4 quarts	3¾ liters
5 quarts	4¾ liters
6 quarts	5½ liters
7 quarts	6½ liters
8 quarts	7½ liters

Converting Pounds to Grams and Kilograms

The numbers in the following table are approximate. To reach the exact number of grams, multiply the number of pounds by 453.6.

POUNDS	GRAMS; KILOGRAMS
1 pound	450 grams
1½ pounds	675 grams
2 pounds	900 grams
2½ pounds	1,125 grams; 1¼ kilograms
3 pounds	1,350 grams
3½ pounds	1,500 grams; 1½ kilograms
4 pounds	1,800 grams
4½ pounds	2 kilograms
5 pounds	2¼ kilograms
5½ pounds	2½ kilograms
6 pounds	2¾ kilograms
6½ pounds	3 kilograms
7 pounds	3¼ kilograms
7½ pounds	3½ kilograms
8 pounds	3¾ kilograms

Converting Fahrenheit to Celsius

The numbers in the following table are approximate. To reach the exact temperature, subtract 32 from the Fahrenheit reading, multiply the number by 5, and then divide by 9.

DEGREES FAHRENHEIT	DEGREES CELSIUS
170°F	77°C
180°F	82°C
190°F	88°C
200°F	95°C
225°F	110°C
250°F	120°C
300°F	150°C
325°F	165°C
350°F	180°C
375°F	190°C
400°F	205°C
425°F	220°C
450°F	230°C
475°F	245°C
500°F	260°C

Converting Inches to Centimeters

The numbers in the following table are approximate. To reach the exact number of centimeters, multiply the number of inches by 2.54.

INCHES	CENTIMETERS
½ inch	1.5 centimeters
1 inch	2.5 centimeters
2 inches	5 centimeters
3 inches	8 centimeters
4 inches	10 centimeters
5 inches	13 centimeters
6 inches	15 centimeters
7 inches	18 centimeters
8 inches	20 centimeters
9 inches	23 centimeters
10 inches	25 centimeters
11 inches	28 centimeters
12 inches	30 centimeters

Appendix B

Measurement Tables

Table of Weights and Measures of Common Ingredients

FOOD	QUANTITY	YIELD
Apples	1 pound	2½ to 3 cups sliced
Avocado	1 pound	1 cup mashed fruit
Bananas	1 medium	1 cup sliced
Bell peppers	1 pound	3 to 4 cups sliced
Blueberries	1 pound	3⅓ cups
Butter	¼ pound (1 stick)	8 tablespoons
Cabbage	1 pound	4 cups packed shredded
Carrots	1 pound	3 cups diced or sliced
Chocolate, bulk	1 ounce	3 tablespoons grated
Chocolate, morsels	12 ounces	2 cups
Cocoa powder	1 ounce	¼ cup
Coconut, flaked	7 ounces	2½ cups
Cream	½ pint (1 cup)	2 cups whipped
Cream cheese	8 ounces	1 cup
Flour	1 pound	4 cups
Lemons	1 medium	3 tablespoons juice
Lemons	1 medium	2 teaspoons zest
Milk	1 quart	4 cups
Molasses	12 ounces	1½ cups
Mushrooms	1 pound	5 cups sliced
Onions	1 medium	½ cup chopped
Peaches	1 pound	2 cups sliced
Peanuts	5 ounces	1 cup
Pecans	6 ounces	1½ cups
Pineapple	1 medium	3 cups diced fruit

Potatoes	1 pound	3 cups sliced
Raisins	1 pound	3 cups
Rice	1 pound	2–2½ cups raw
Spinach	1 pound	¾ cup cooked
Squash, summer	1 pound	3½ cups sliced
Strawberries	1 pint	1½ cups sliced
Sugar, brown	1 pound	2¼ cups packed
Sugar, confectioners'	1 pound	4 cups
Sugar, granulated	1 pound	2¼ cups
Tomatoes	1 pound	1½ cups pulp
Walnuts	4 ounces	1 cup

Table of Liquid Measurements	
Pinch	Less than ⅛ teaspoon
3 teaspoons	1 tablespoon
2 tablespoons	1 fluid ounce
8 tablespoons	½ cup
2 cups	1 pint
1 quart	2 pints
1 gallon	4 quarts

Index